This Zodiac Coloring Book Belongs To:

_____

_____

_____

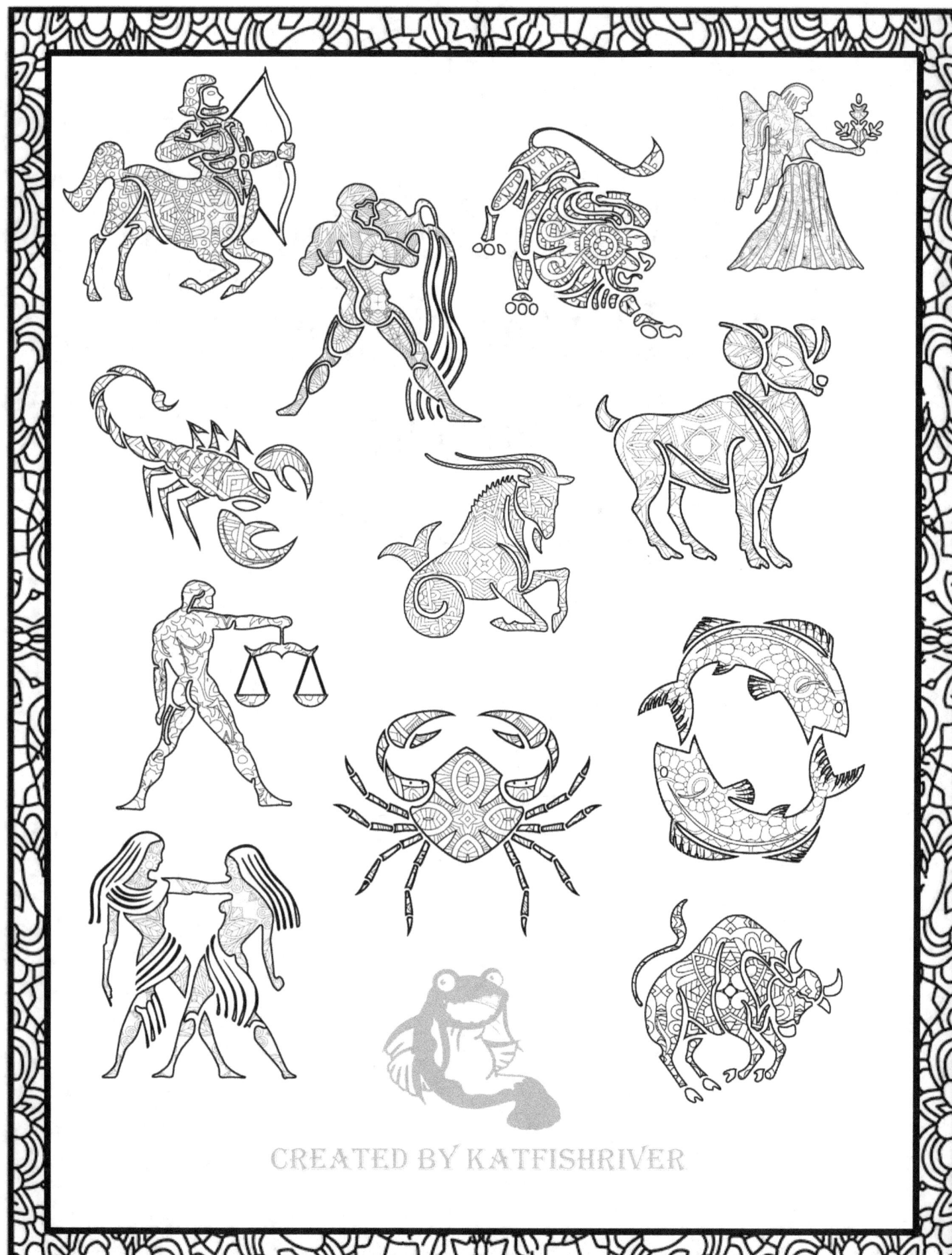

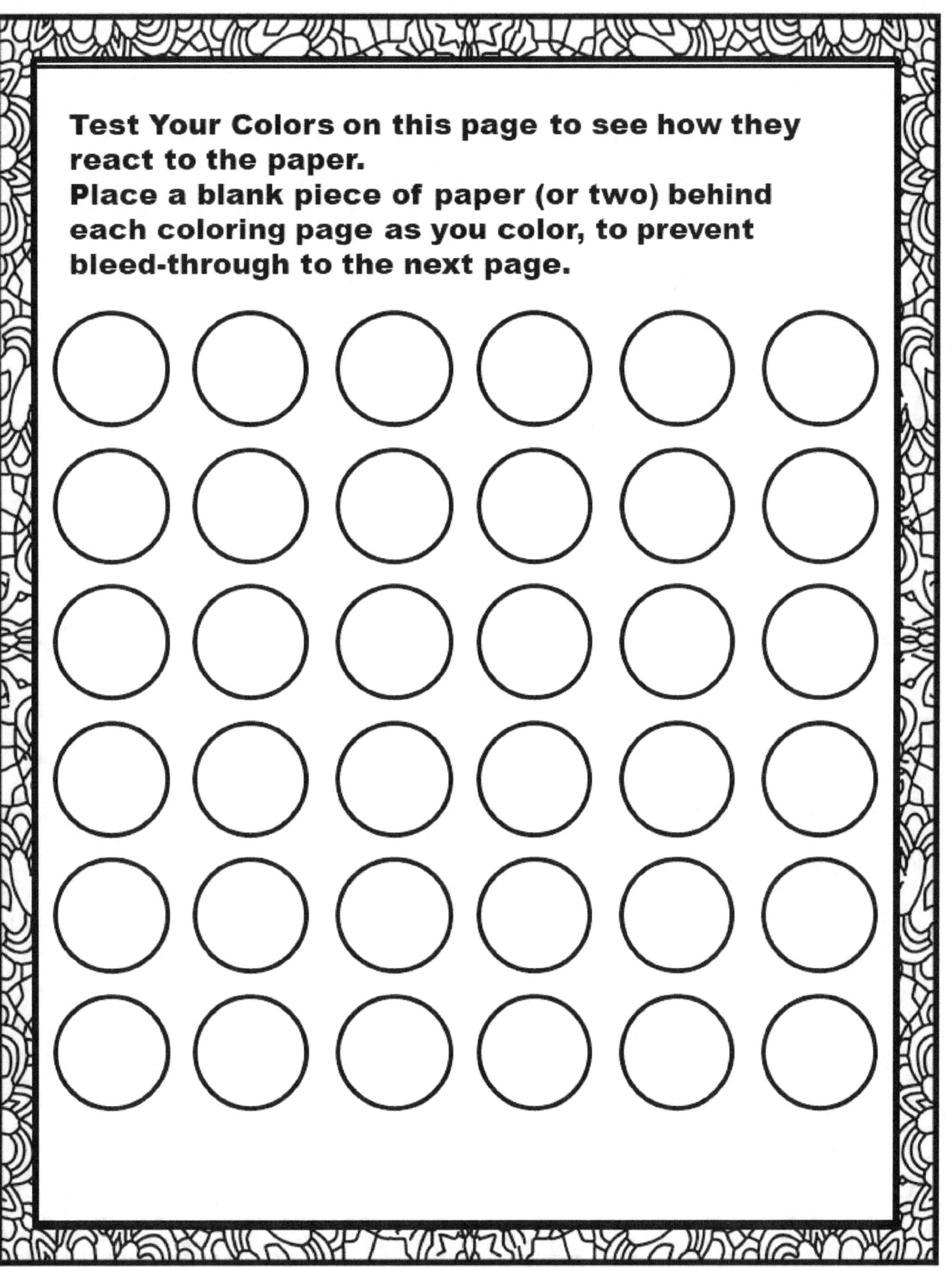

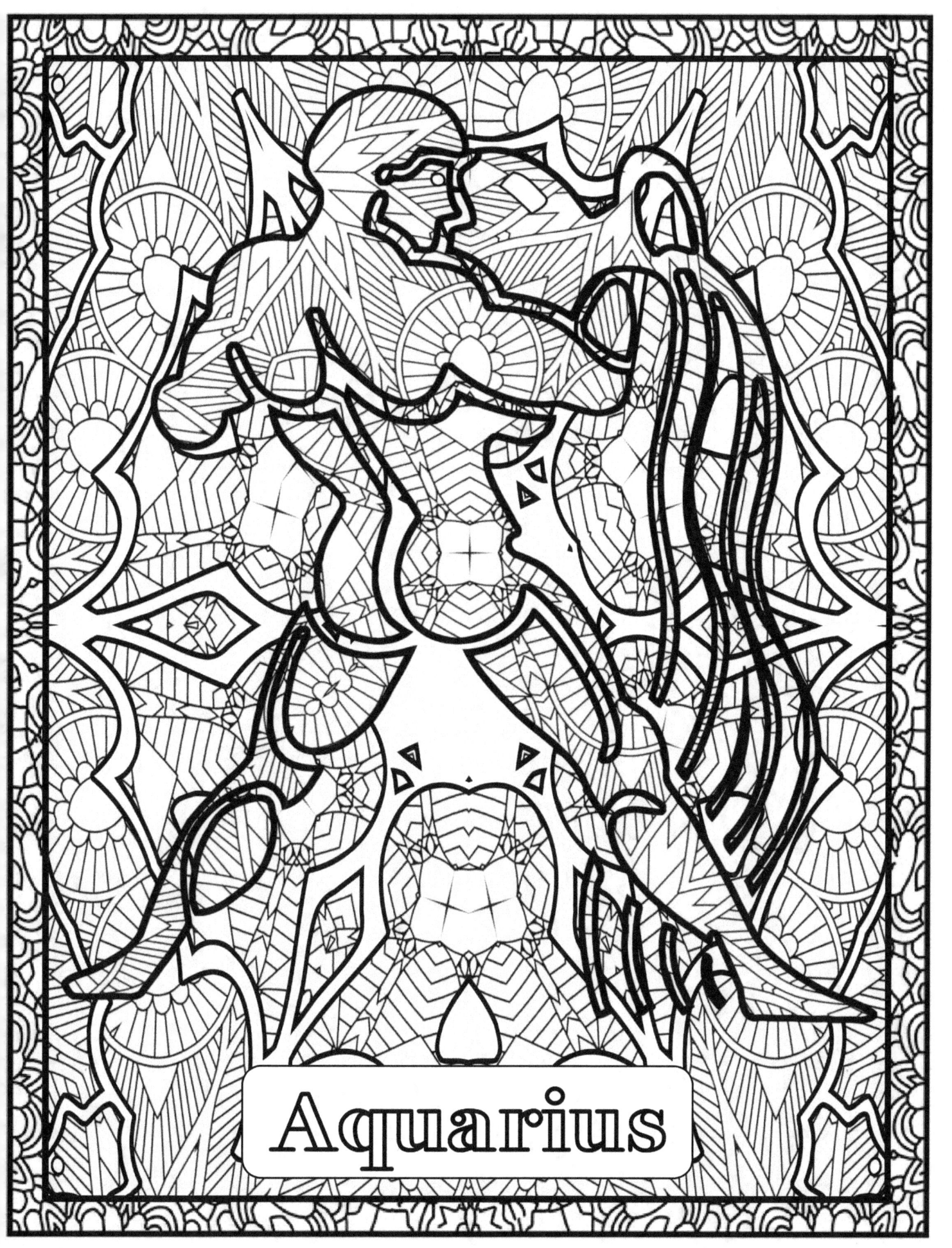

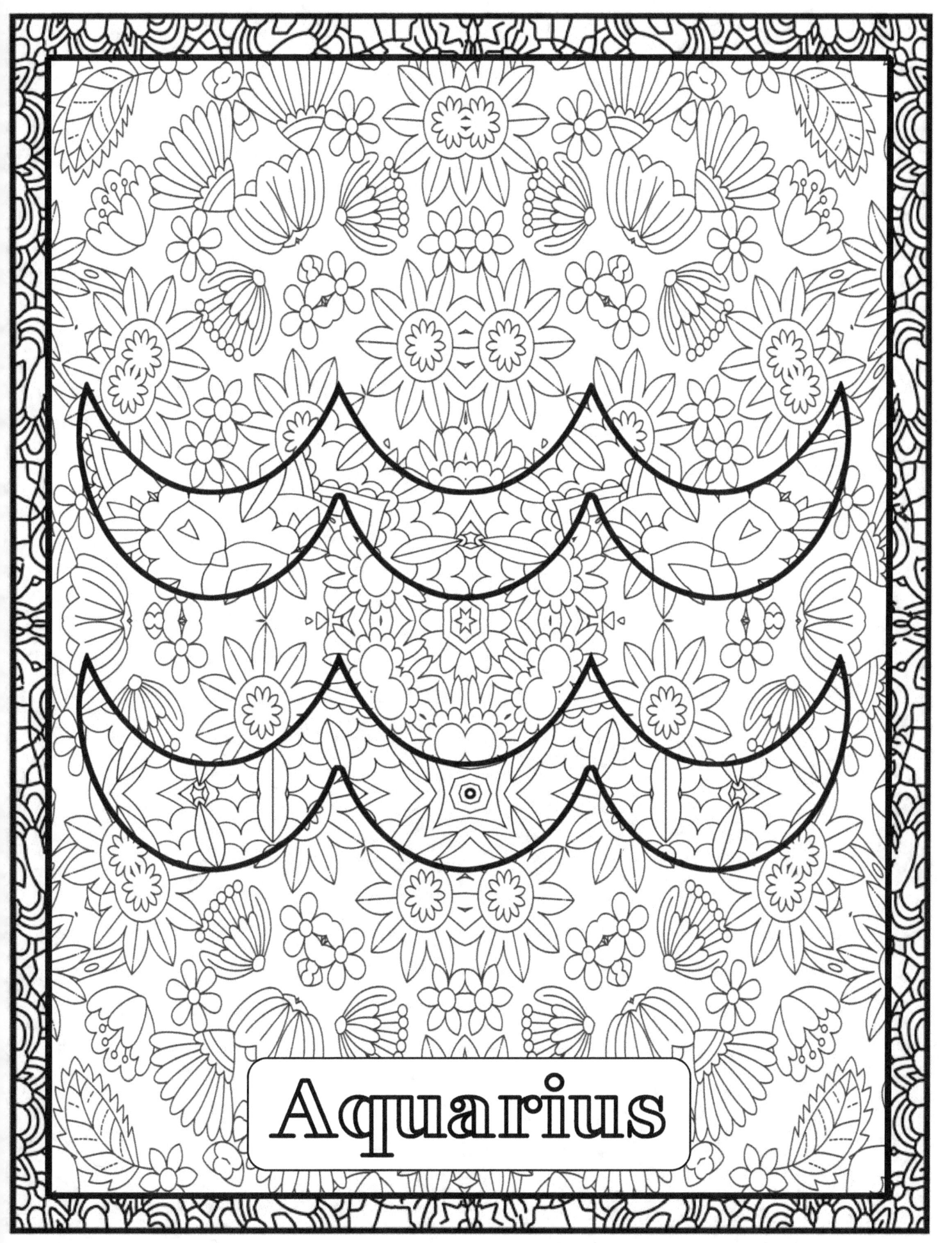

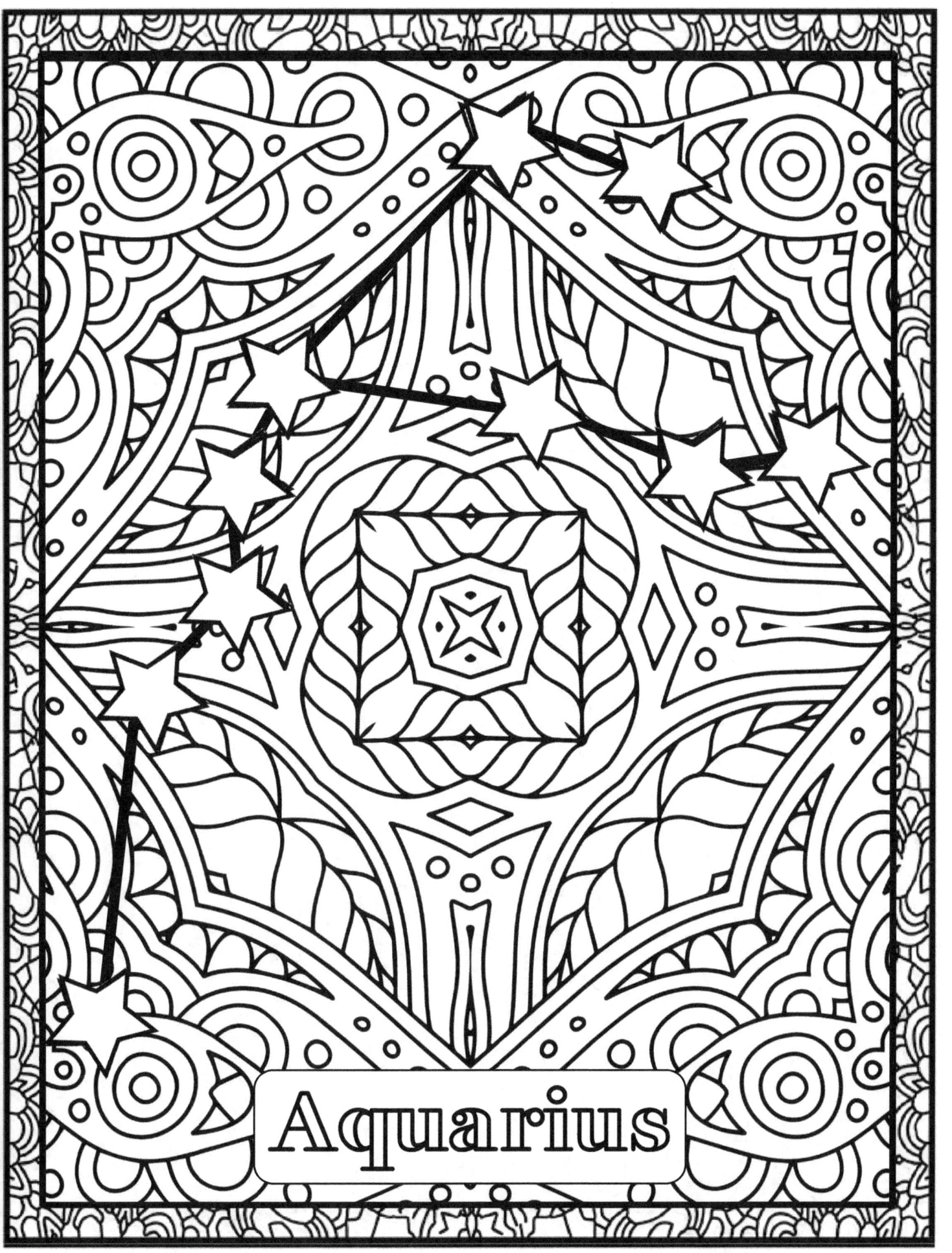

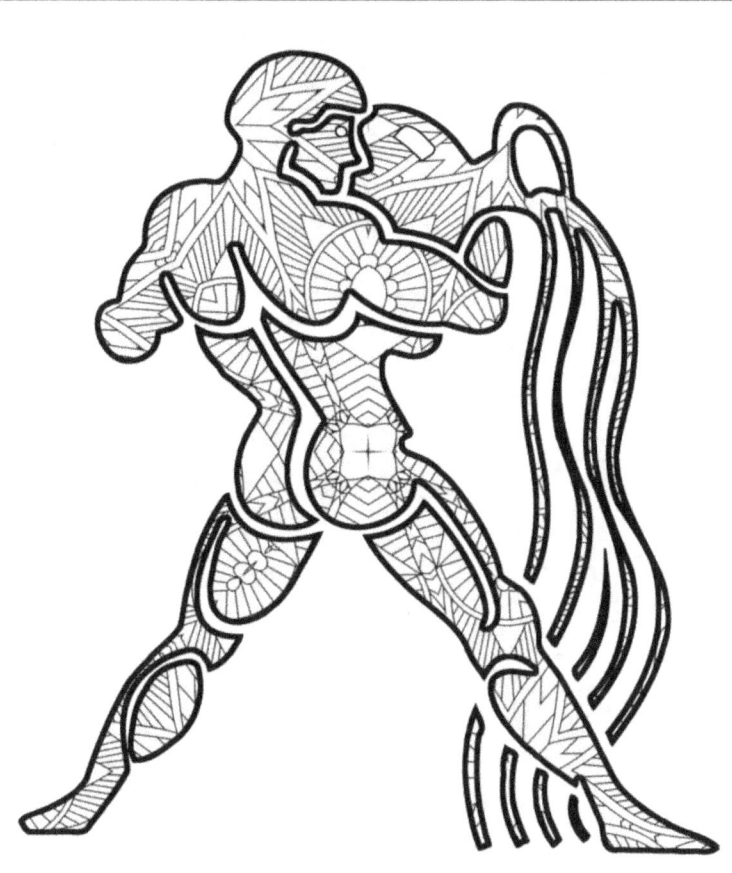

Aquarius
Jan 20 – Feb 18

Deep, Imaginative, Original and Uncompromising

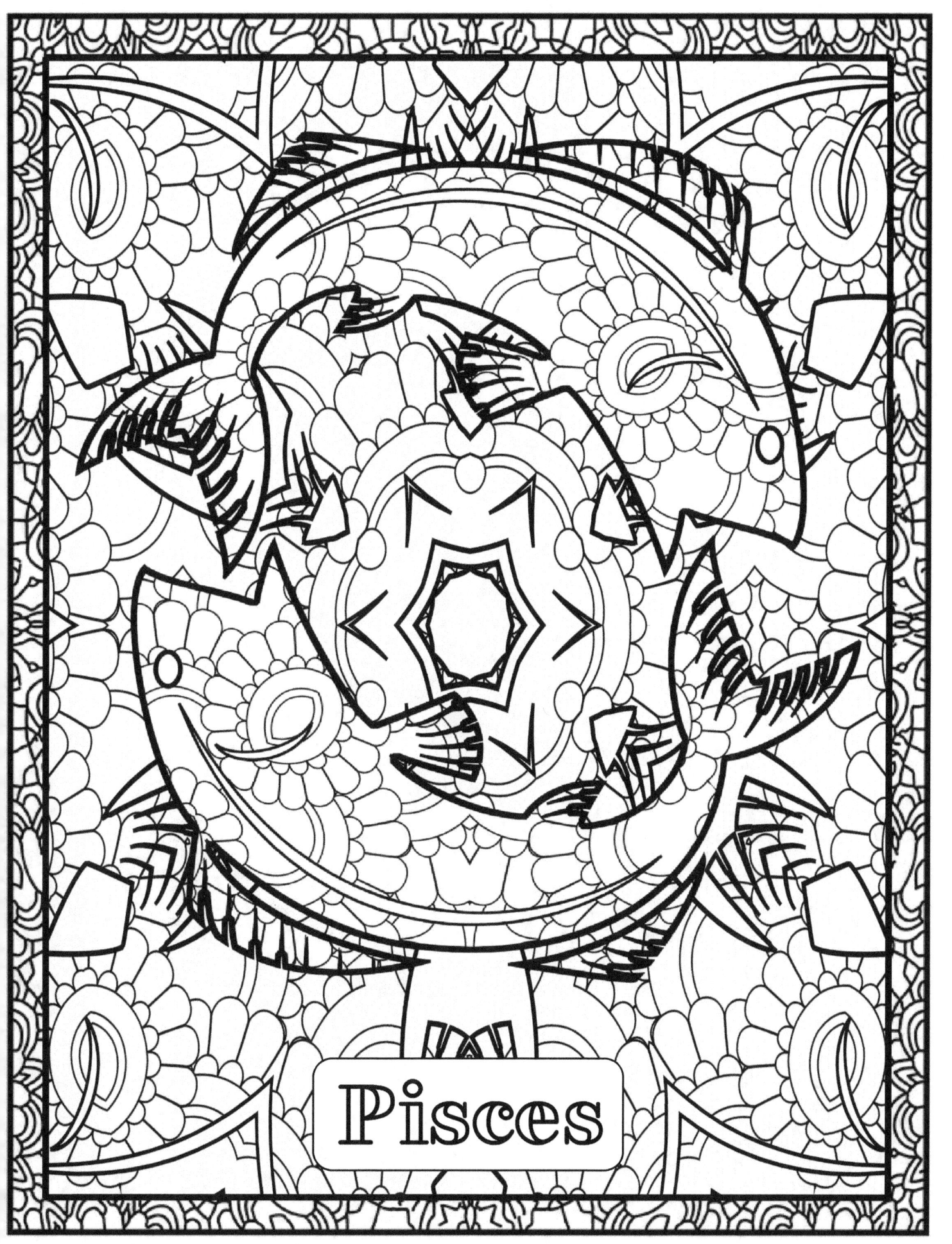

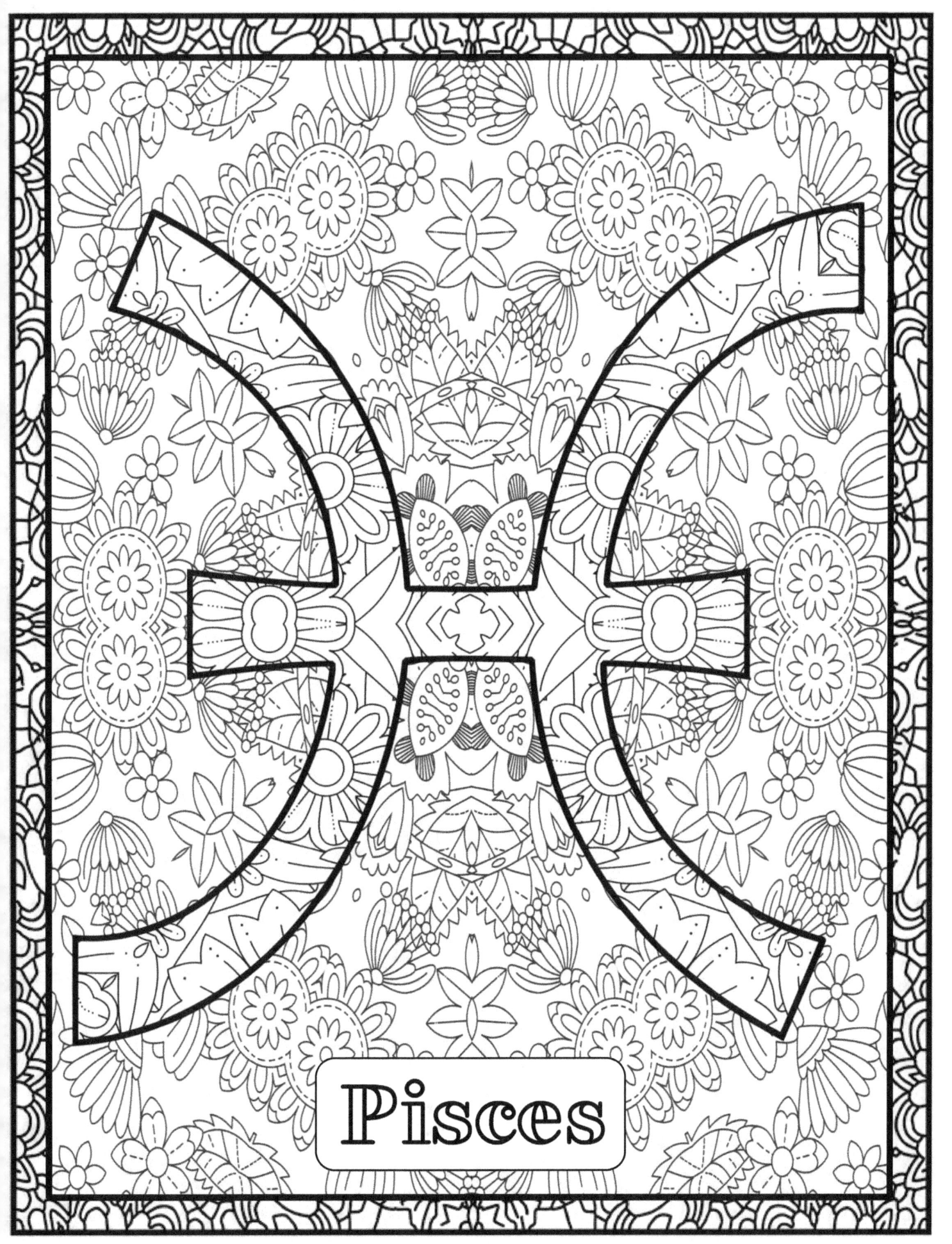

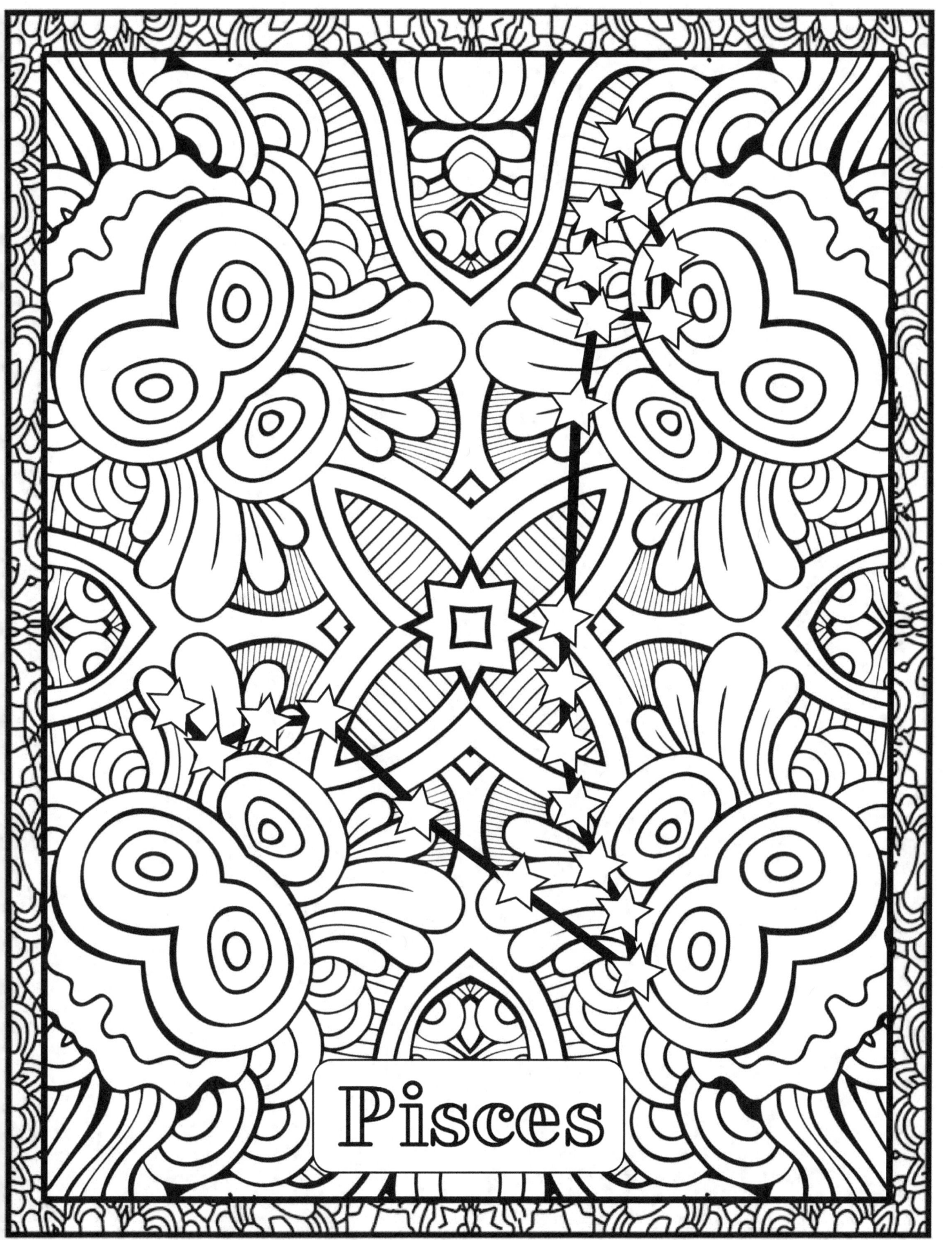

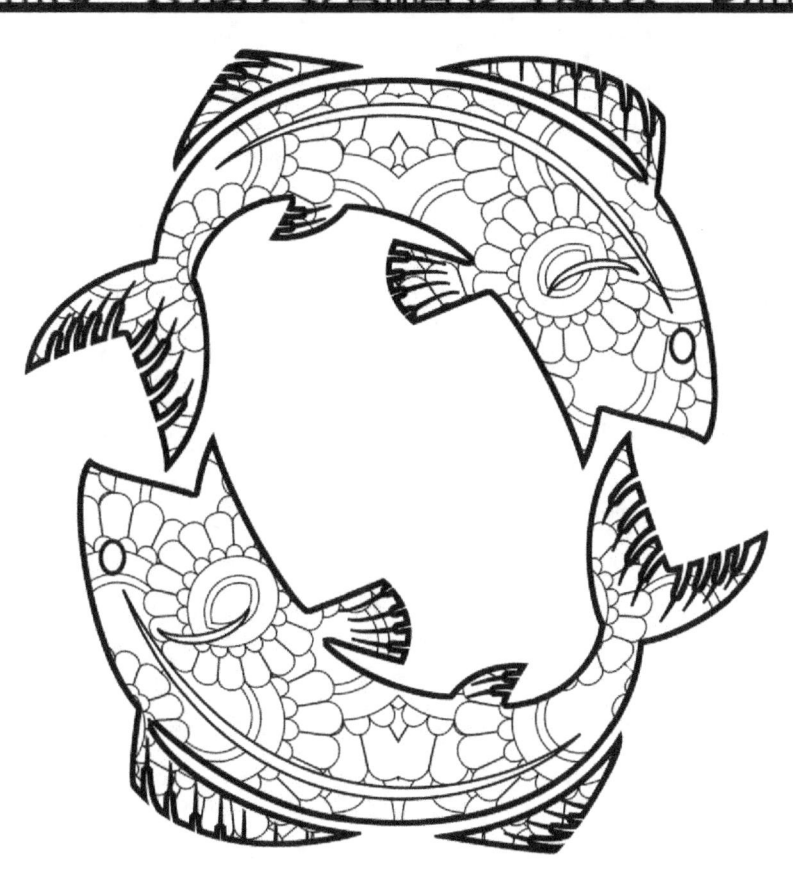

Pisces

Feb 19 – Mar 20

Affectionate, Empathic, Wise

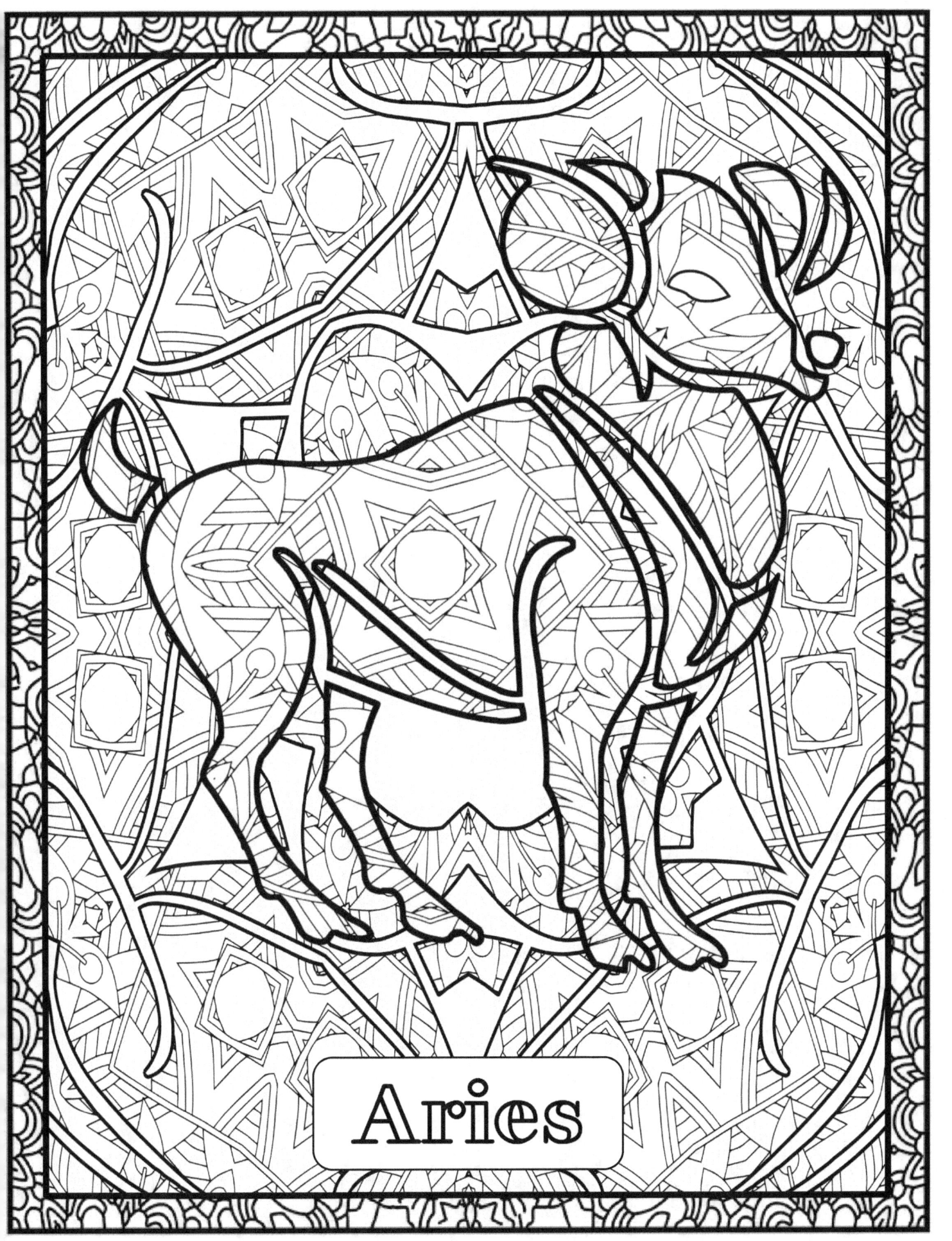

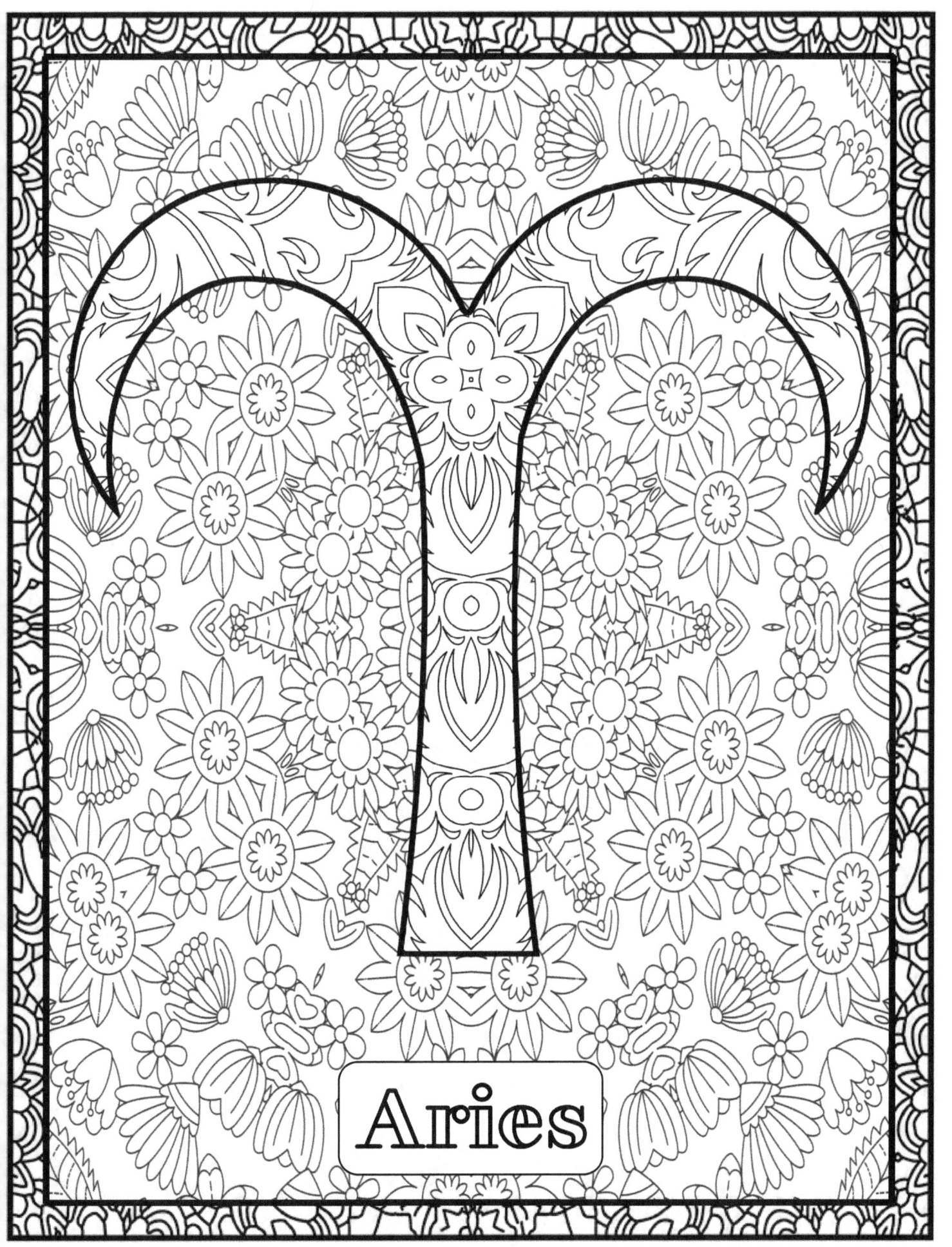

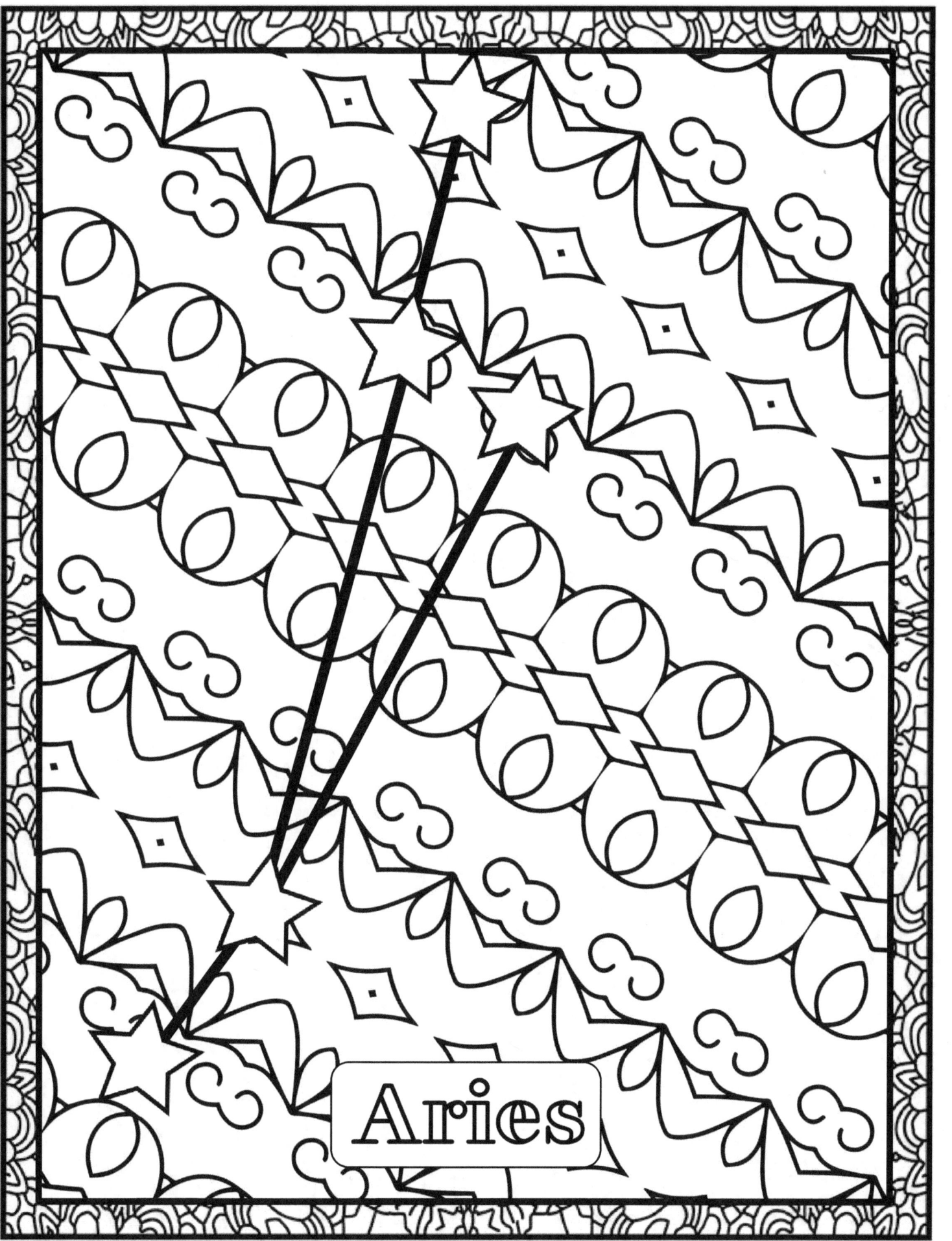

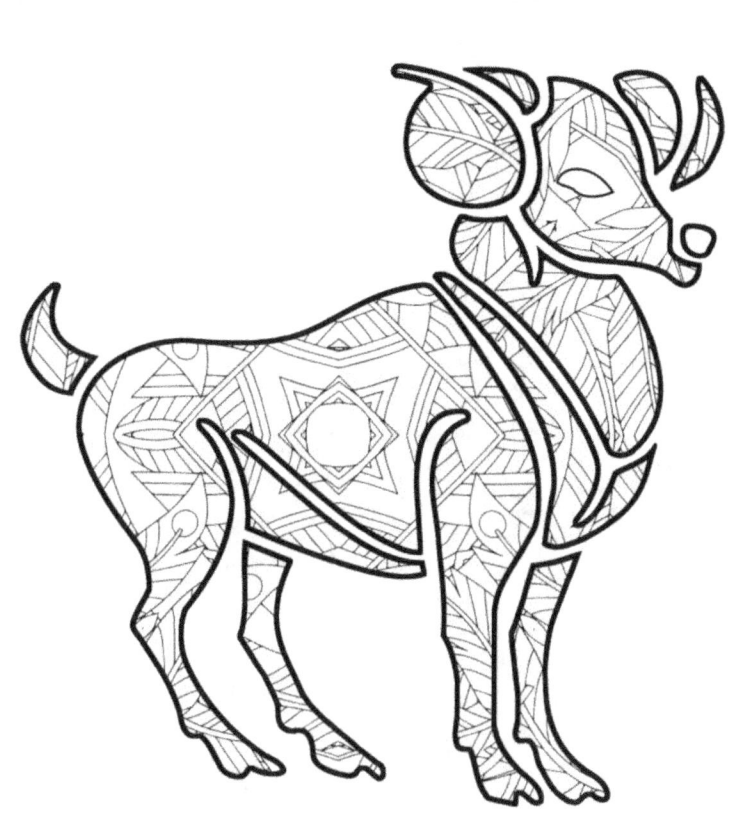

Aries
Mar 21 – Apr 19

Eager, Dynamic, Quick and Competitive

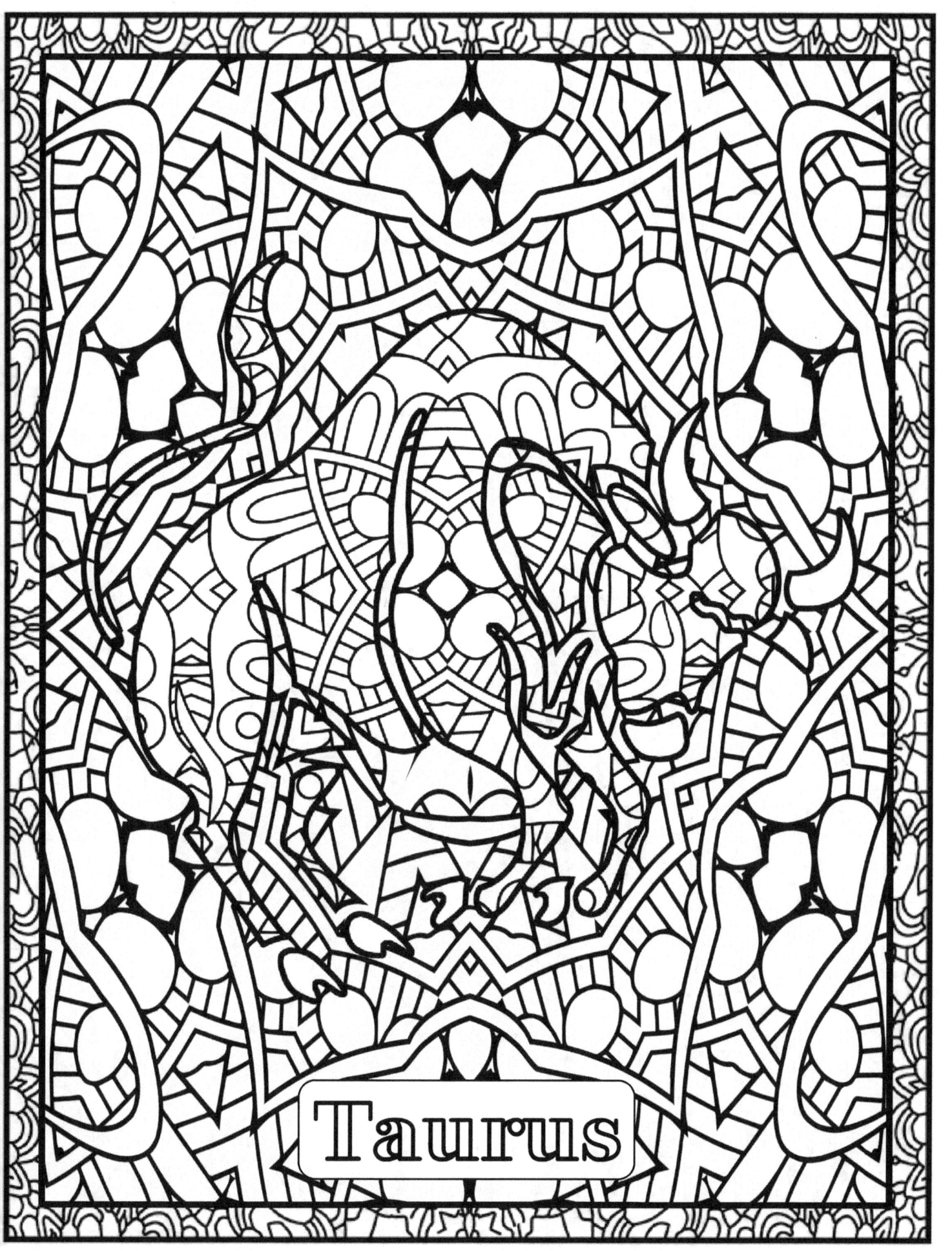

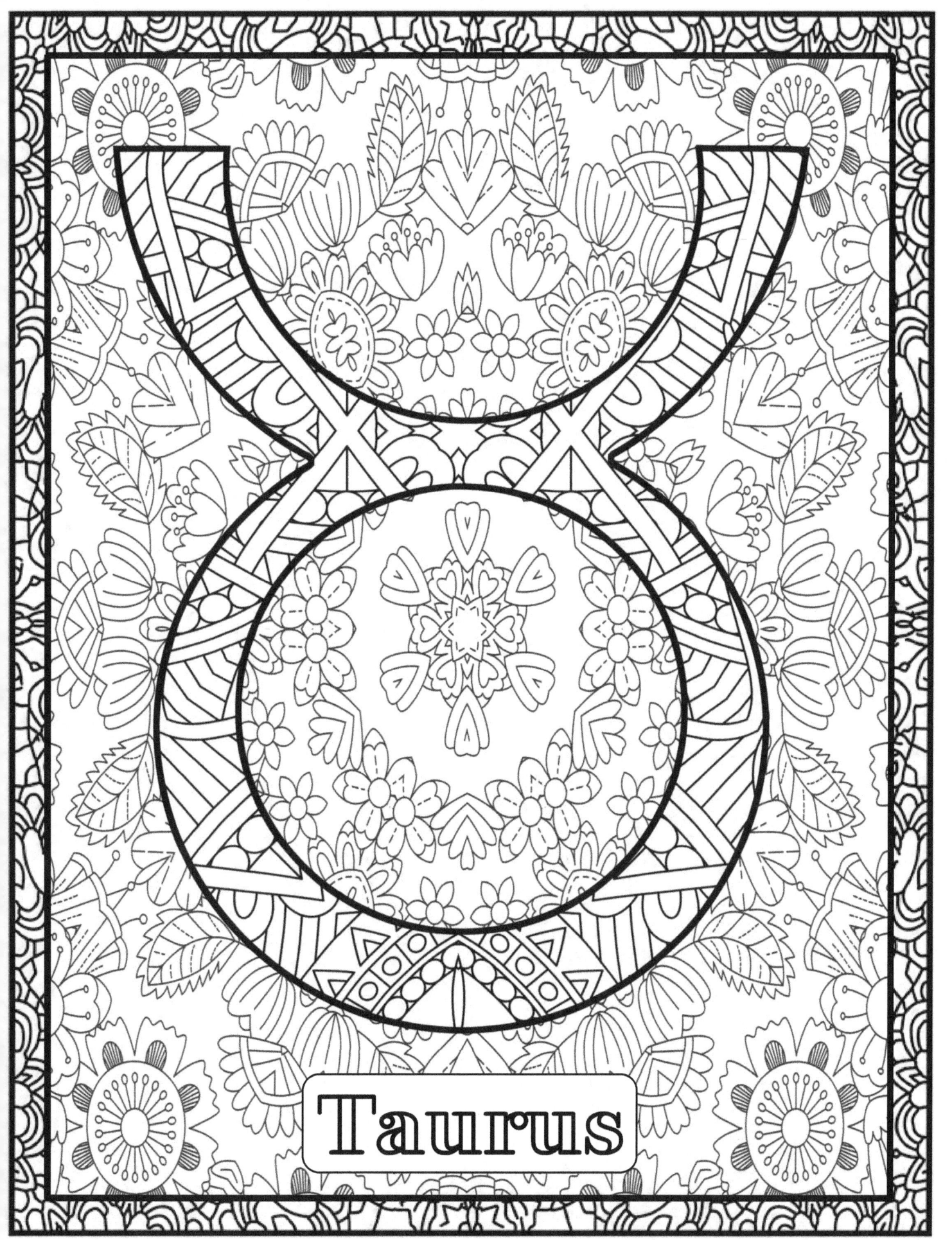

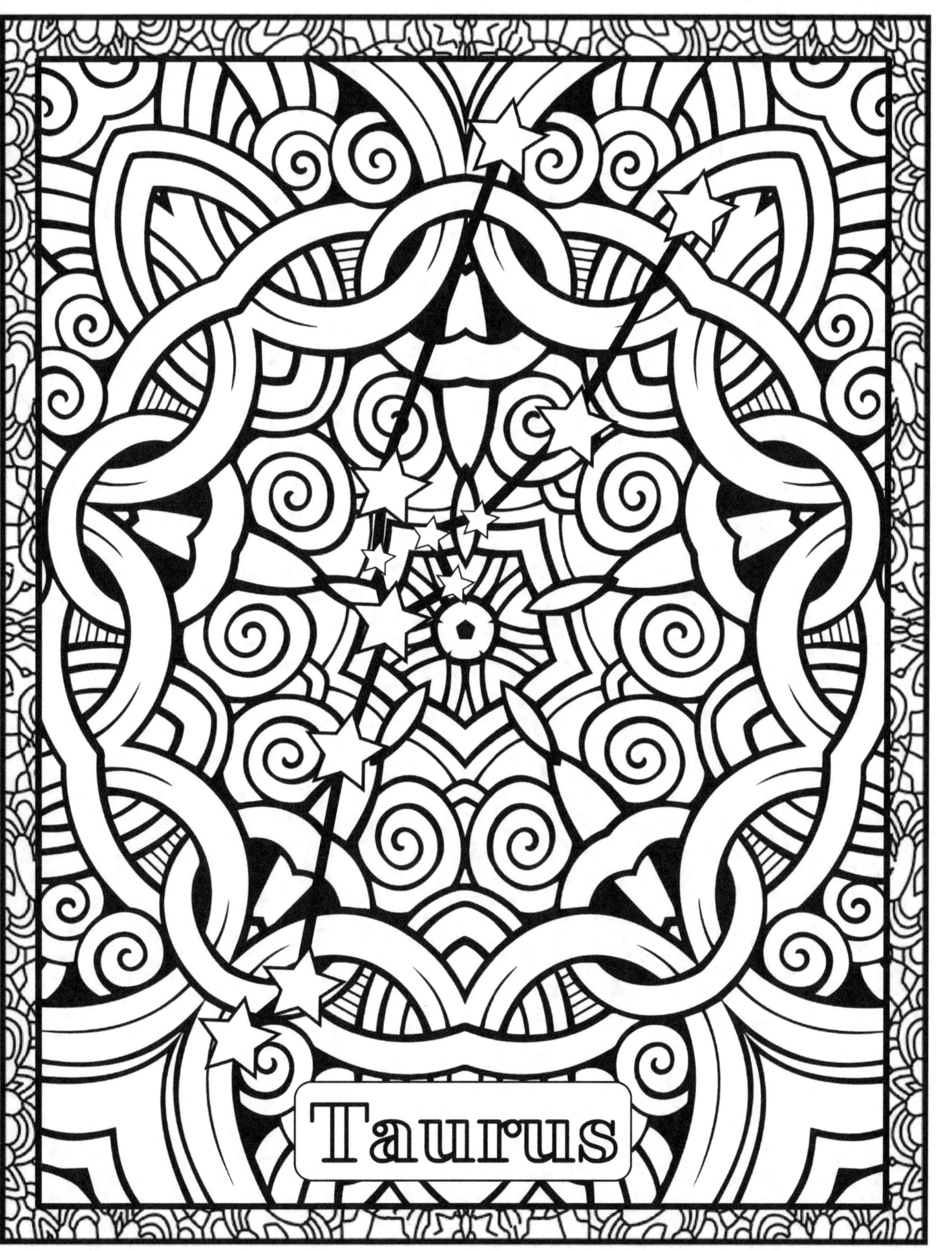

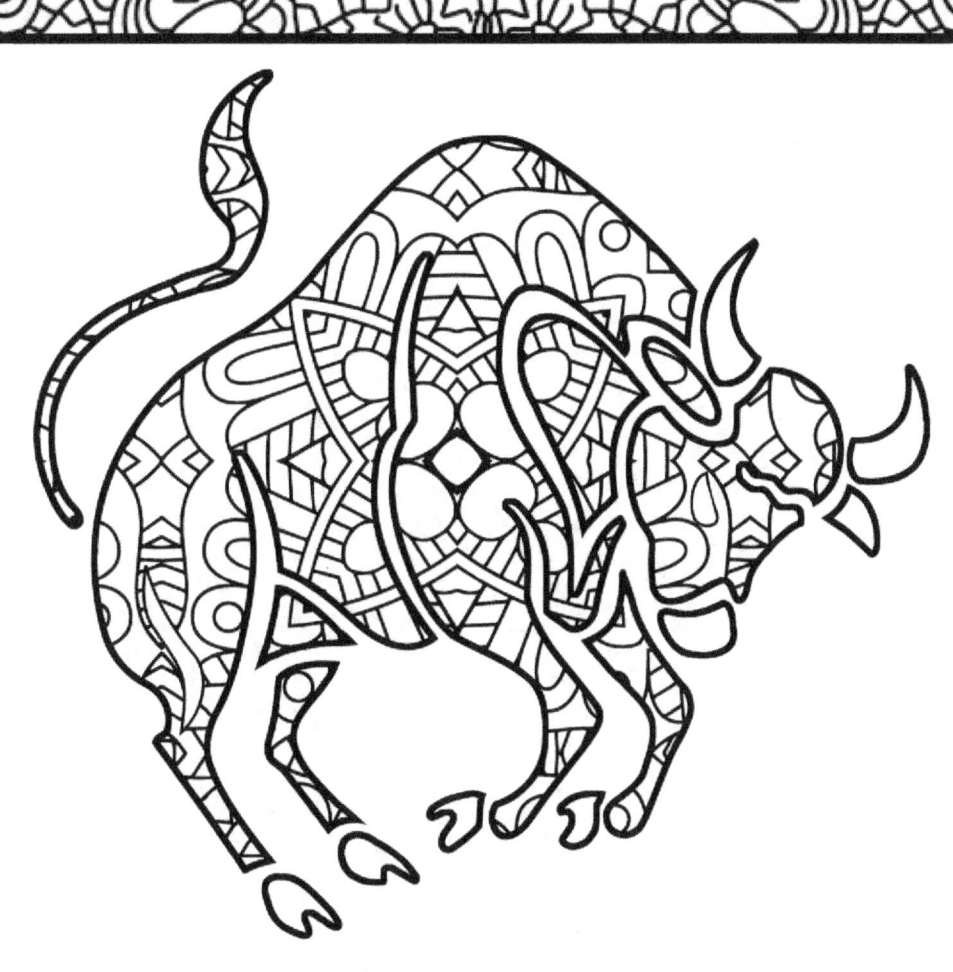

Taurus
Apr 20 – May 20

Strong, Dependable, Sensual and Creative

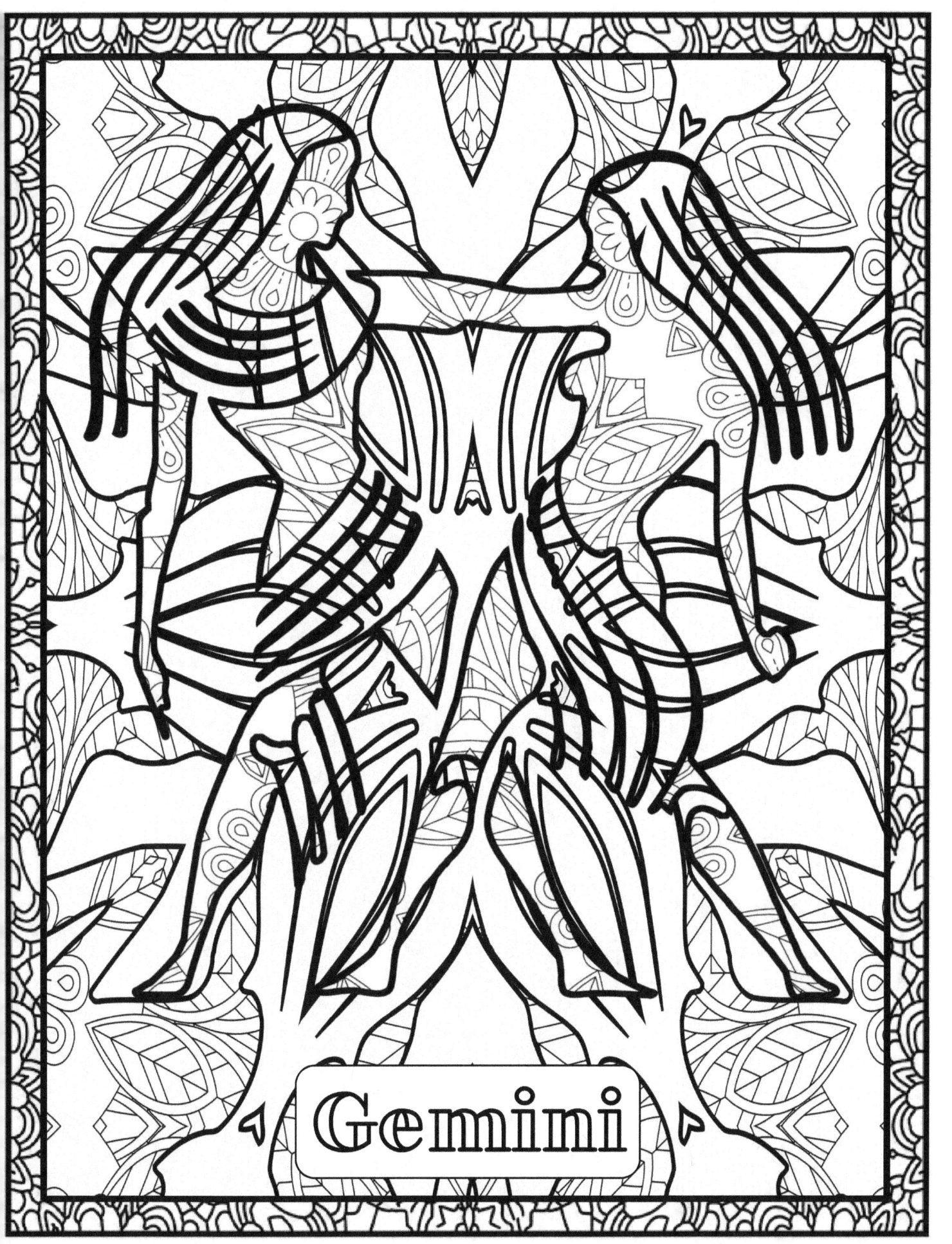

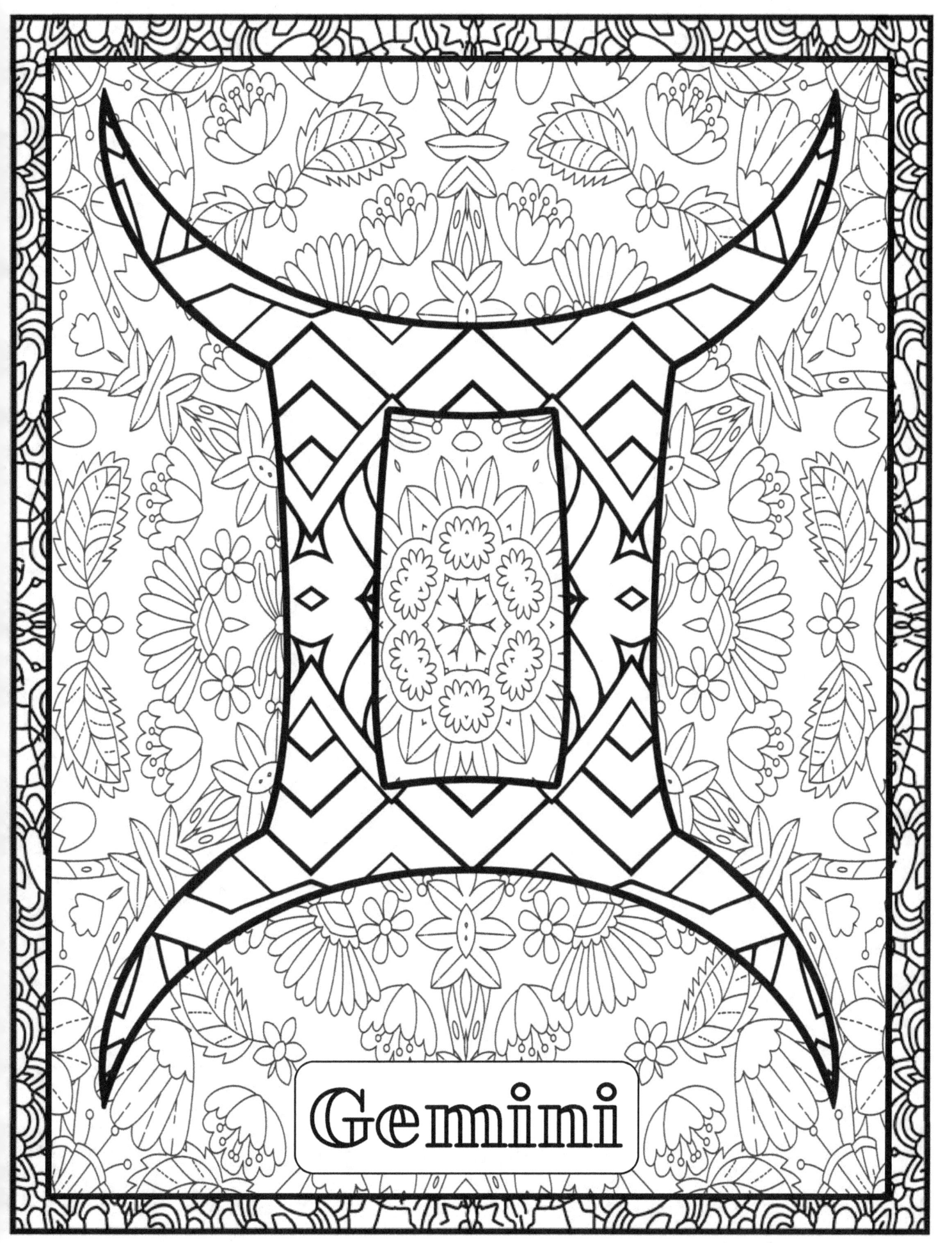

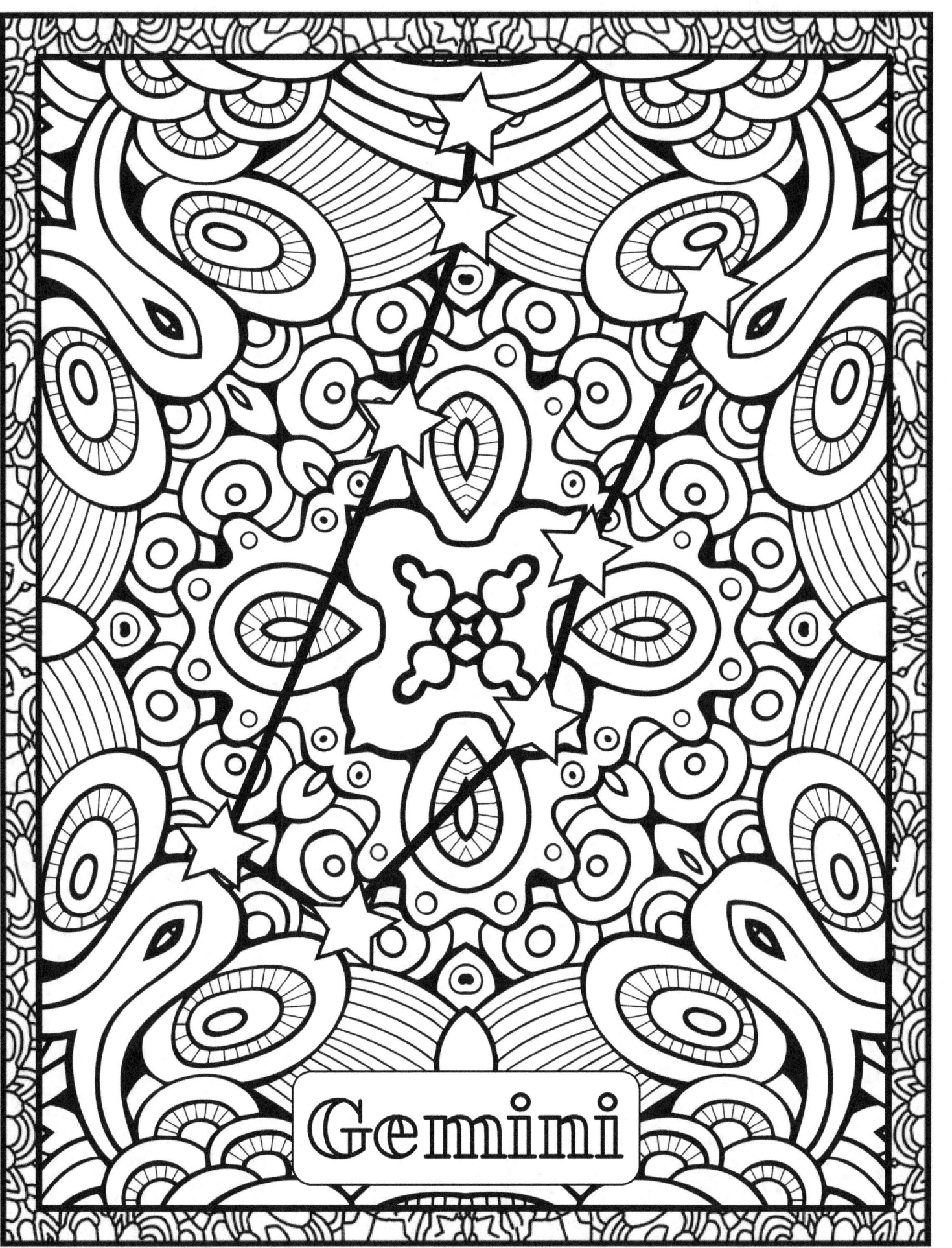

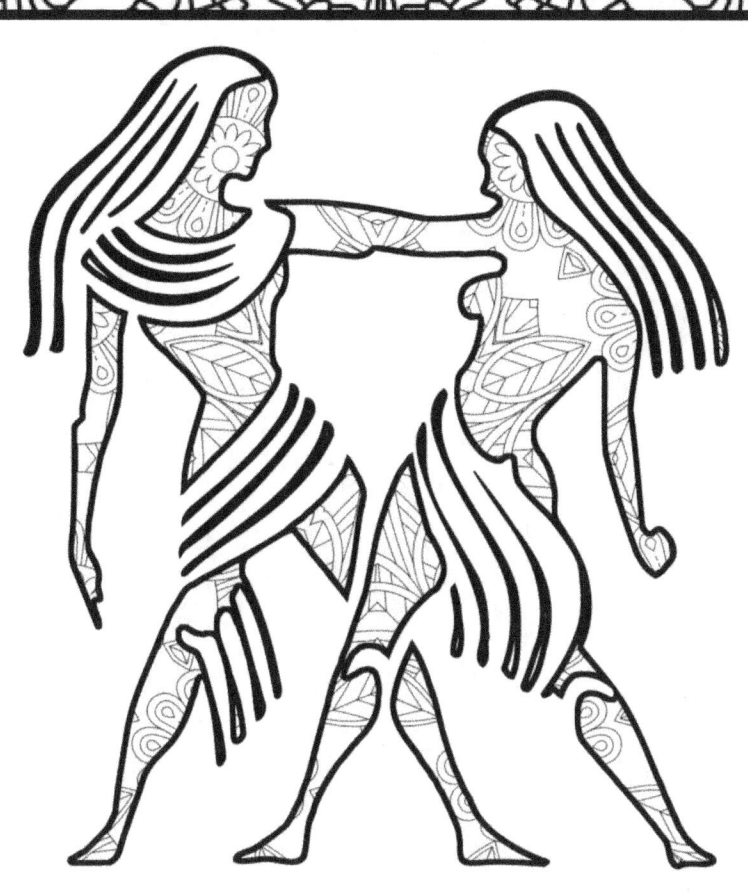

Gemini

May 21 – Jun 20

Versatile, Expressive, Curious and Kind

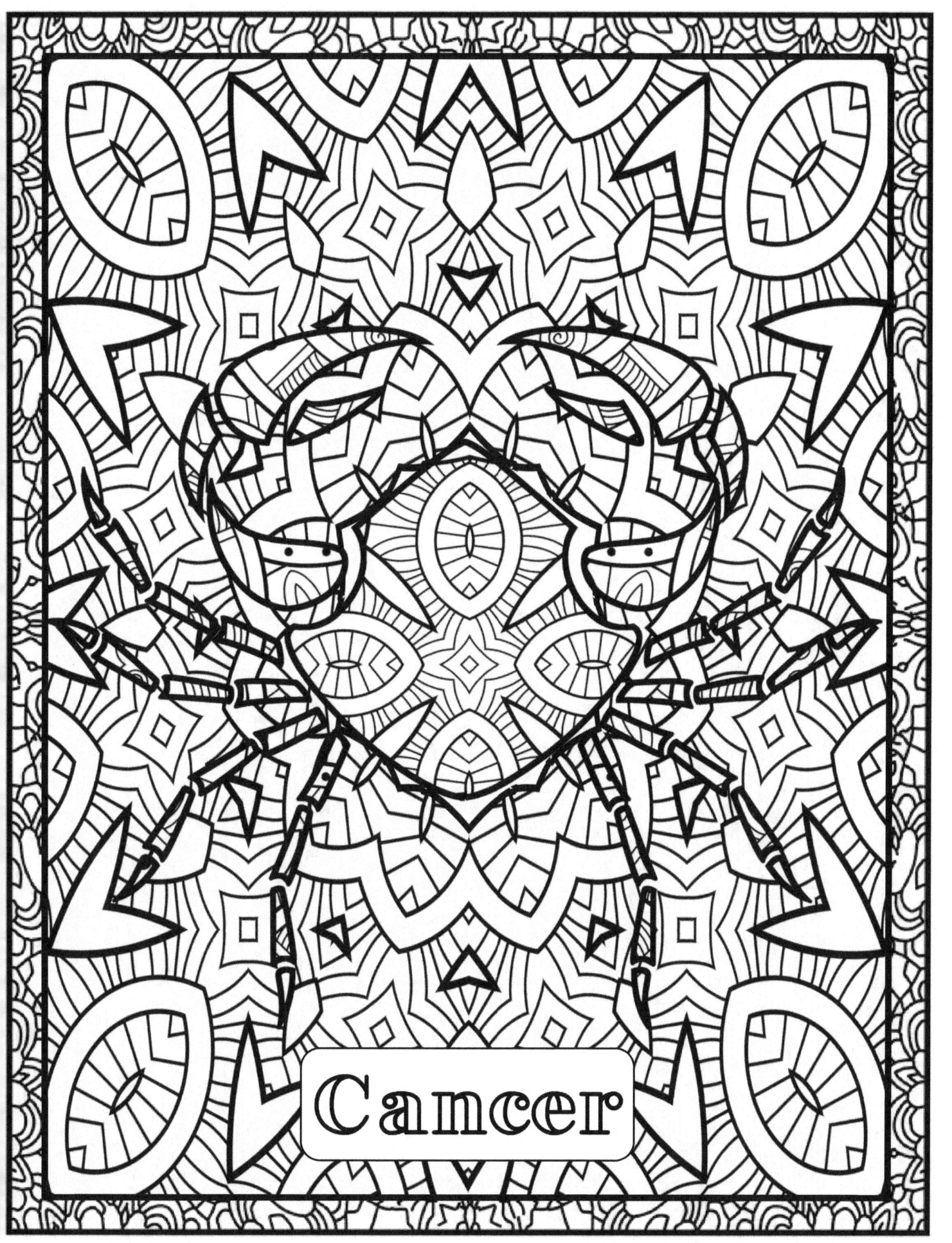

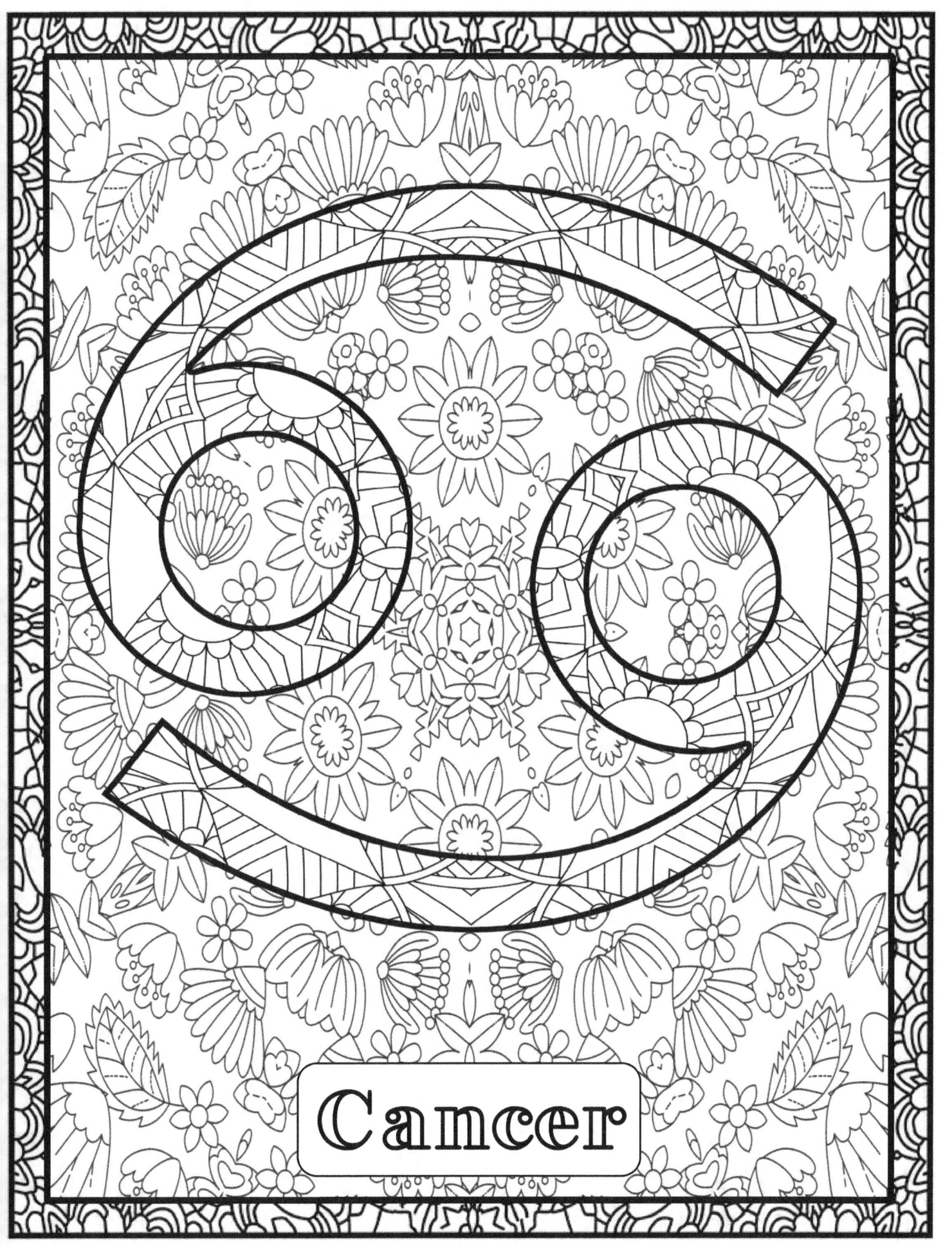

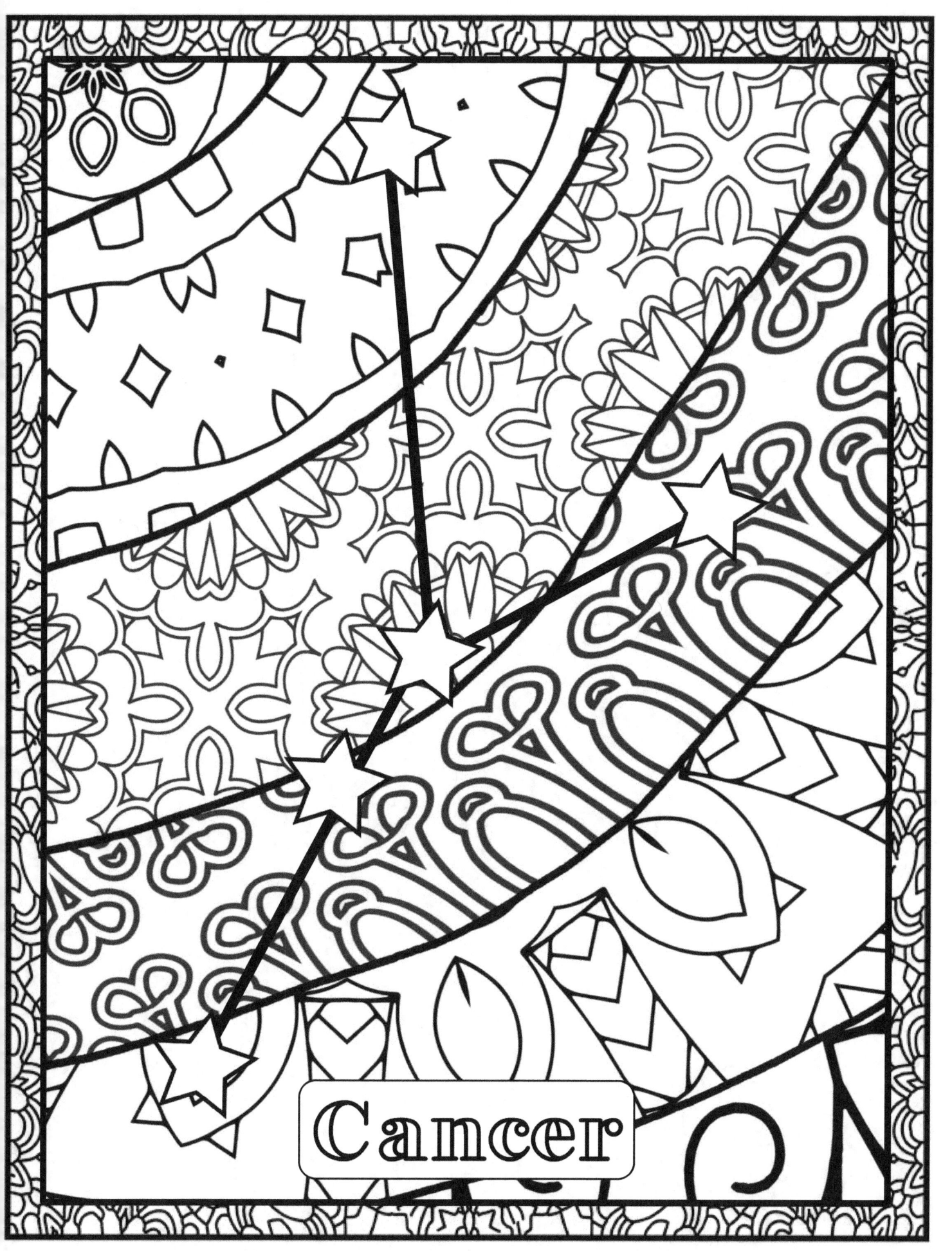

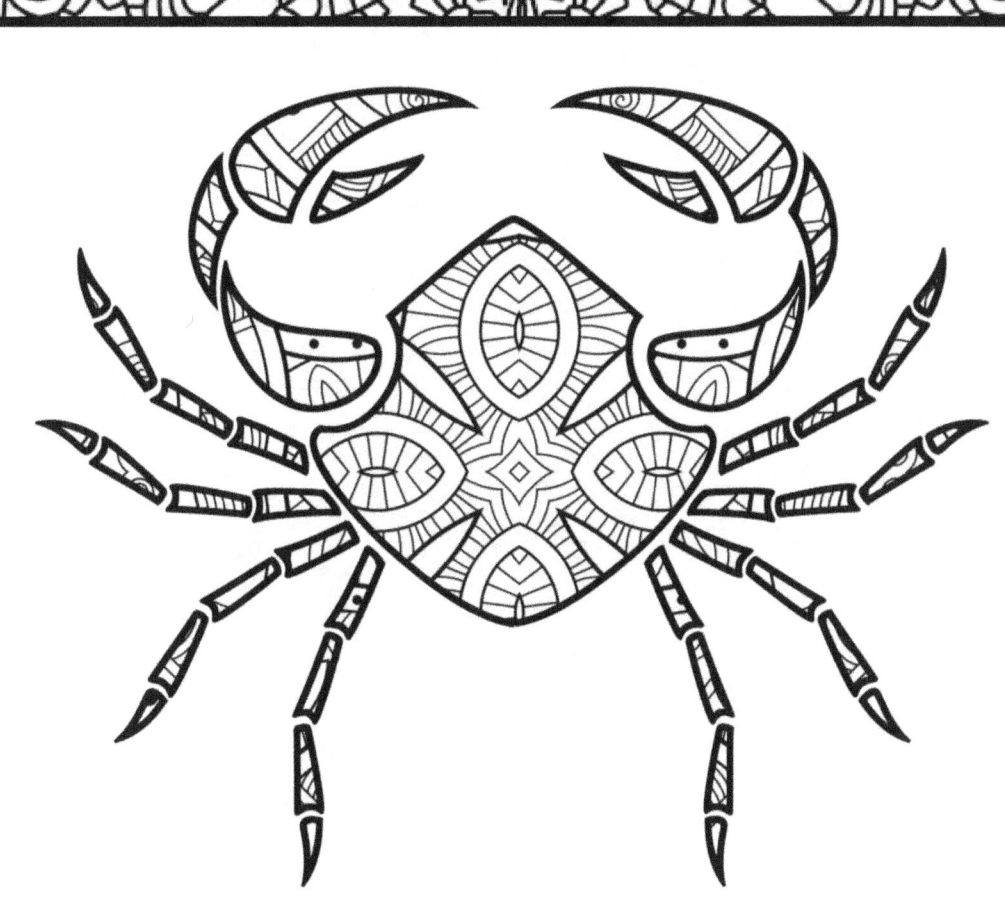

Cancer
Jun 21 – Jul 22

Intuitive, Sentimental,
Compassionate and
Protective

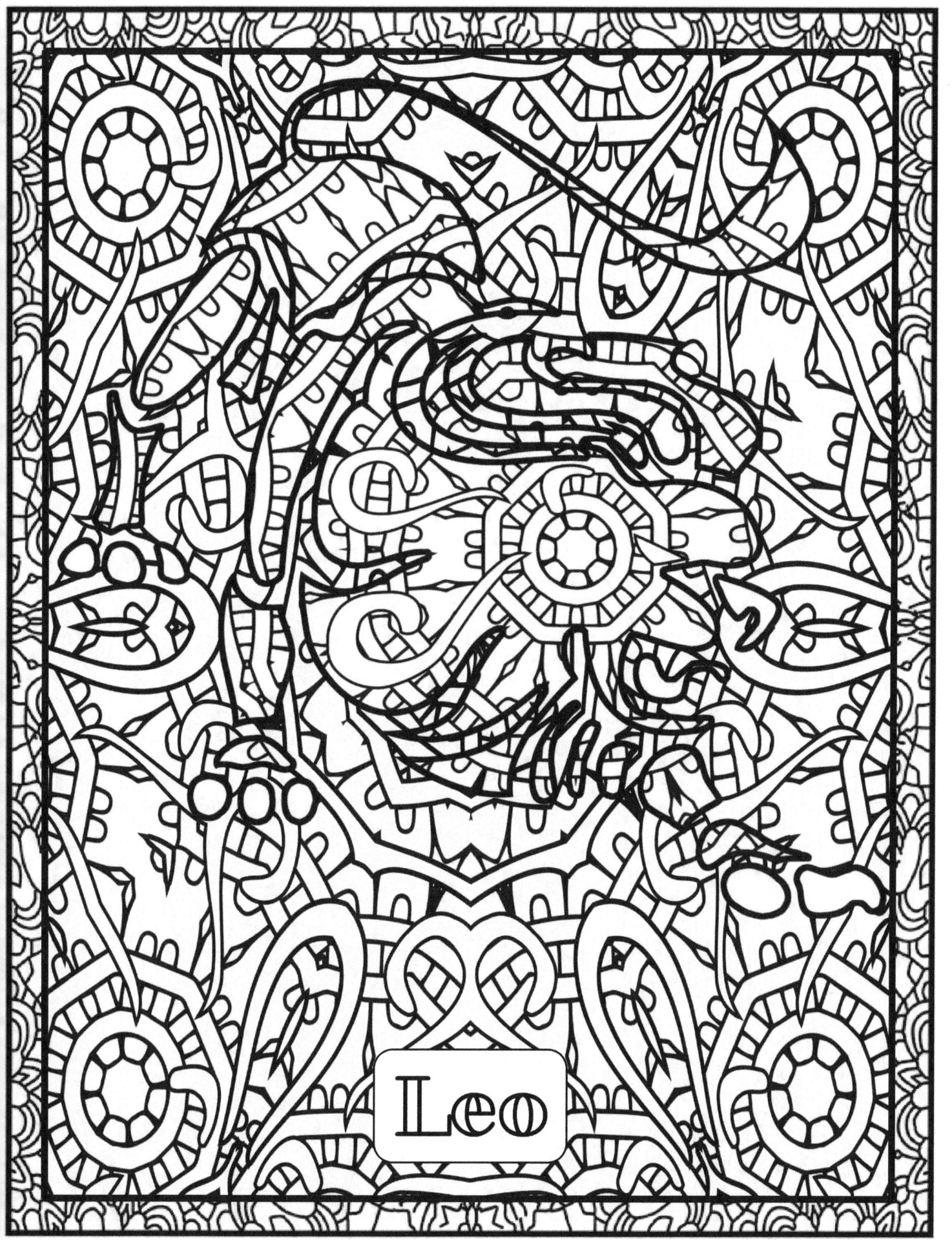

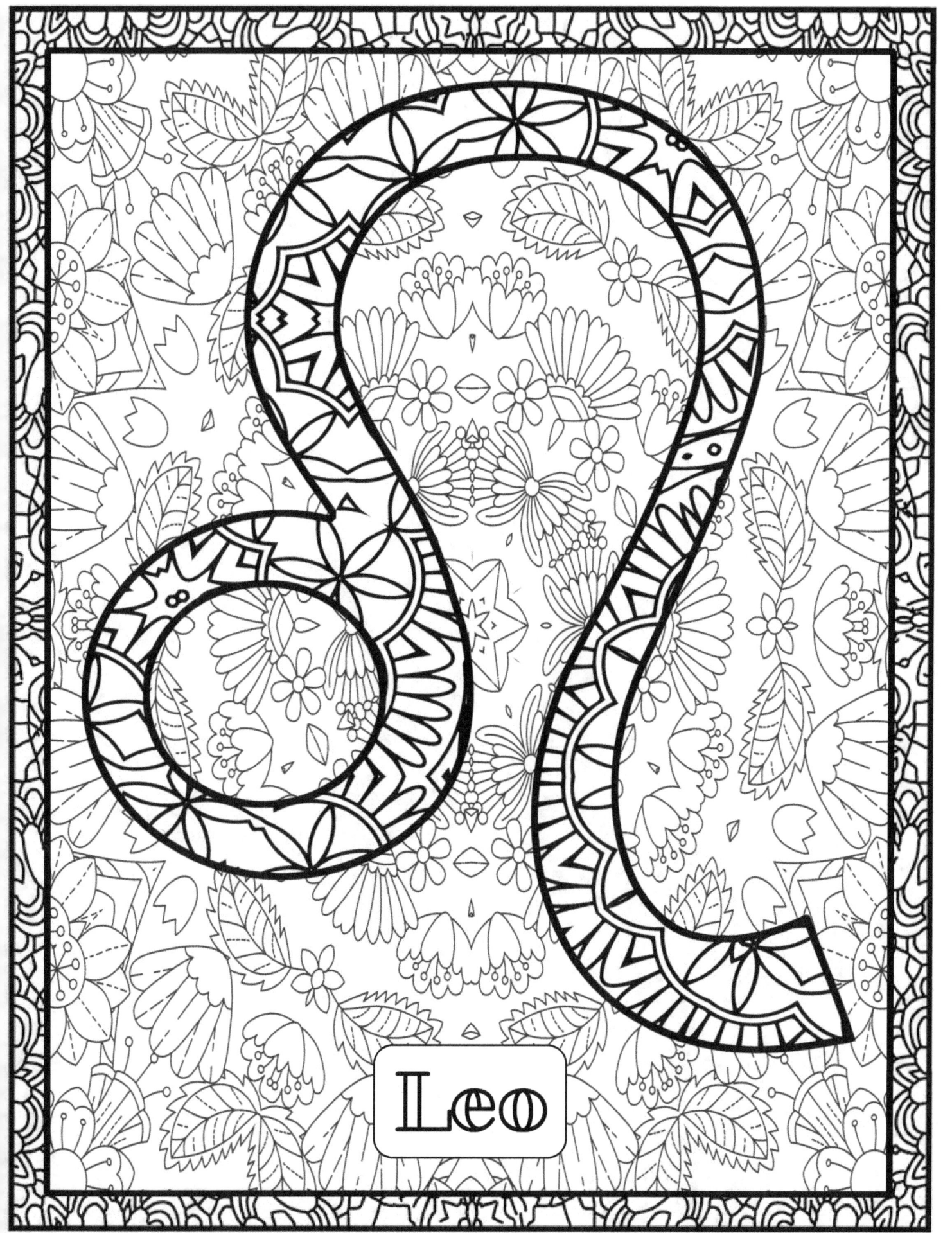

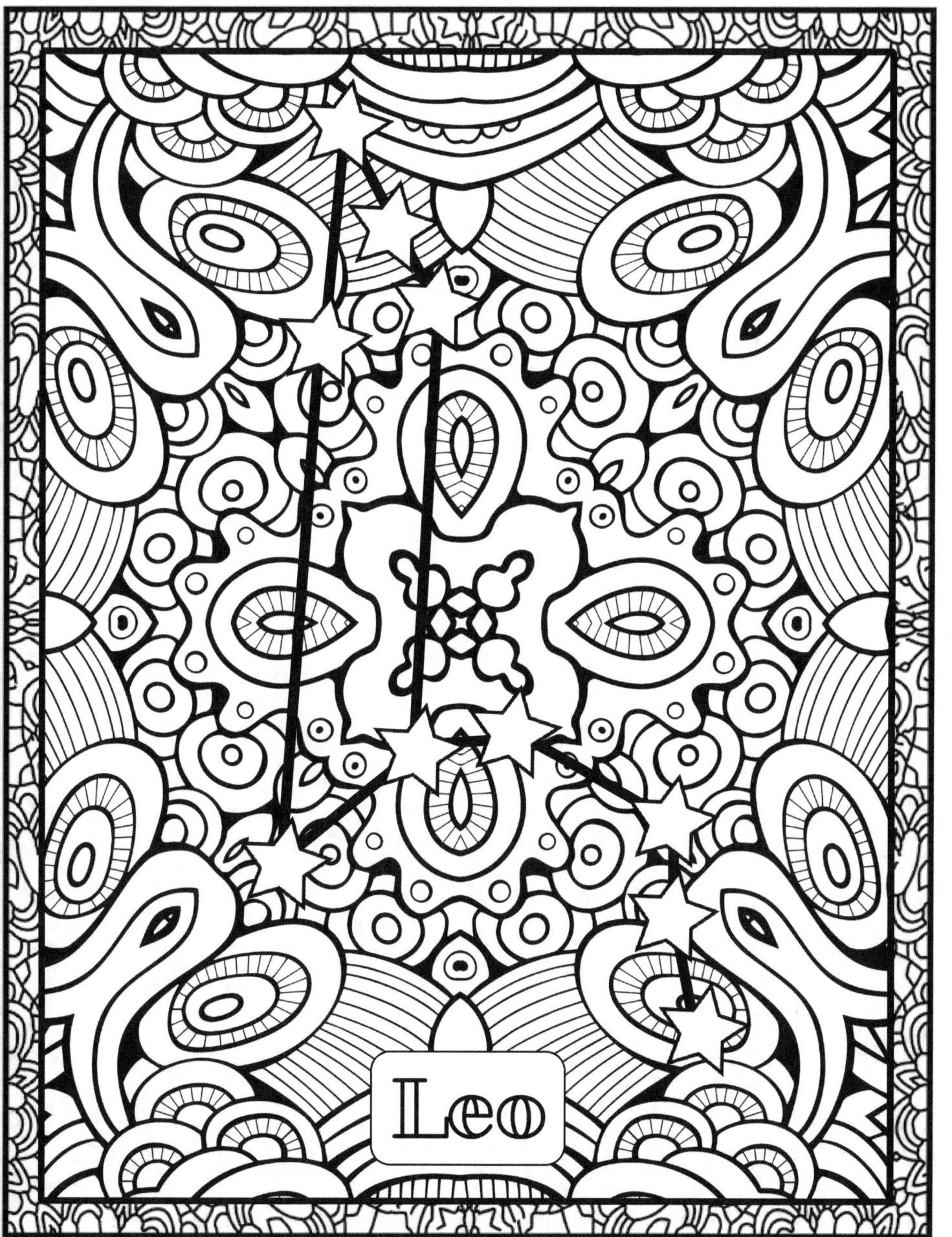

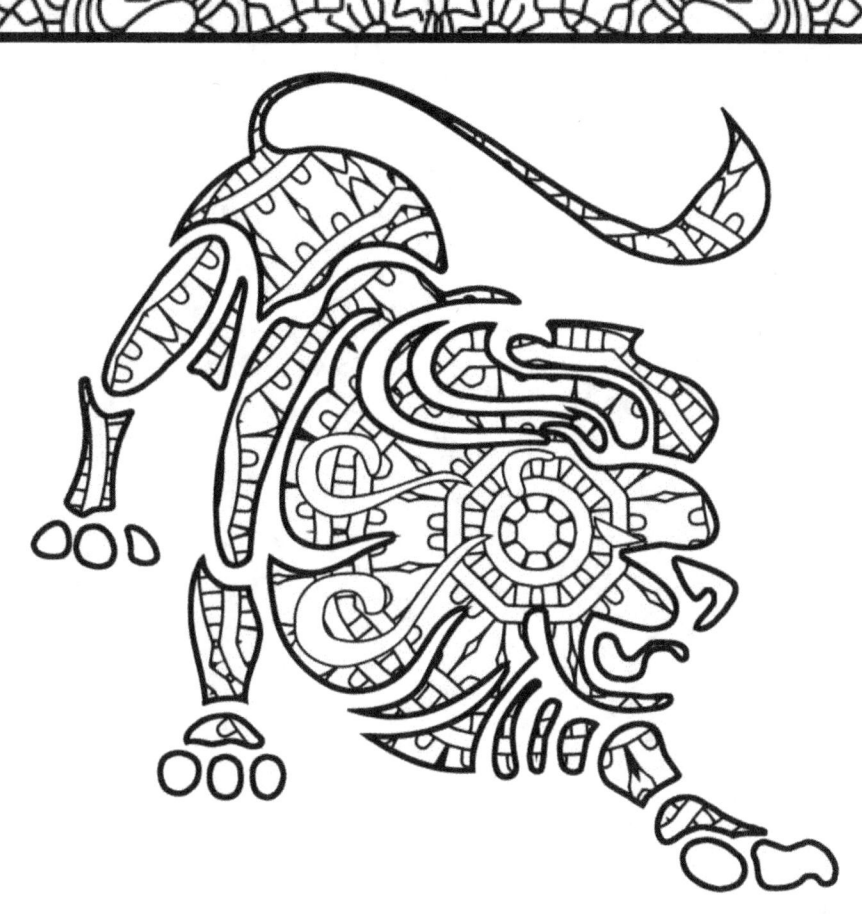

Leo
Jul 23 — Aug 22

Dramatic, Outgoing, Fiery and Self-Assured

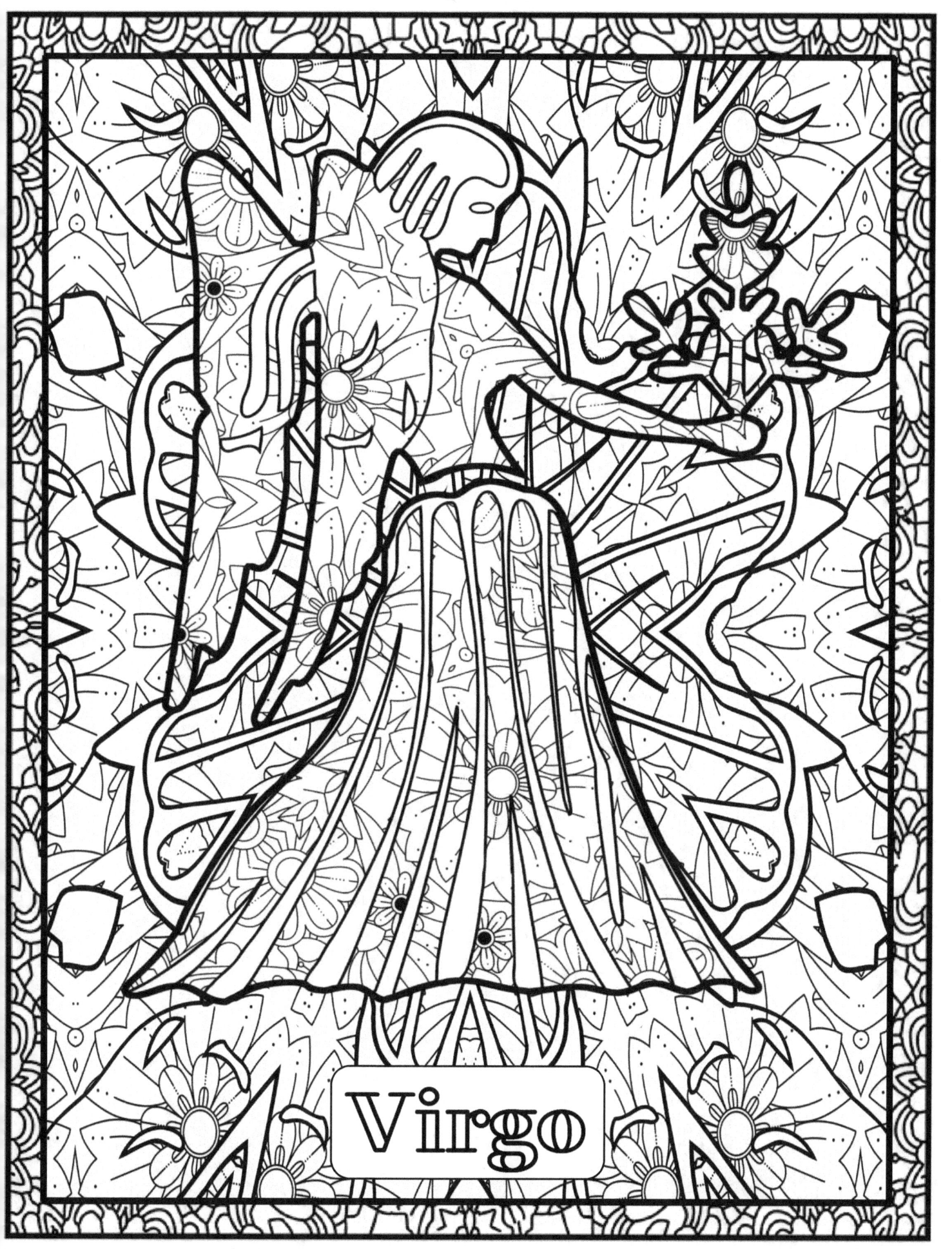

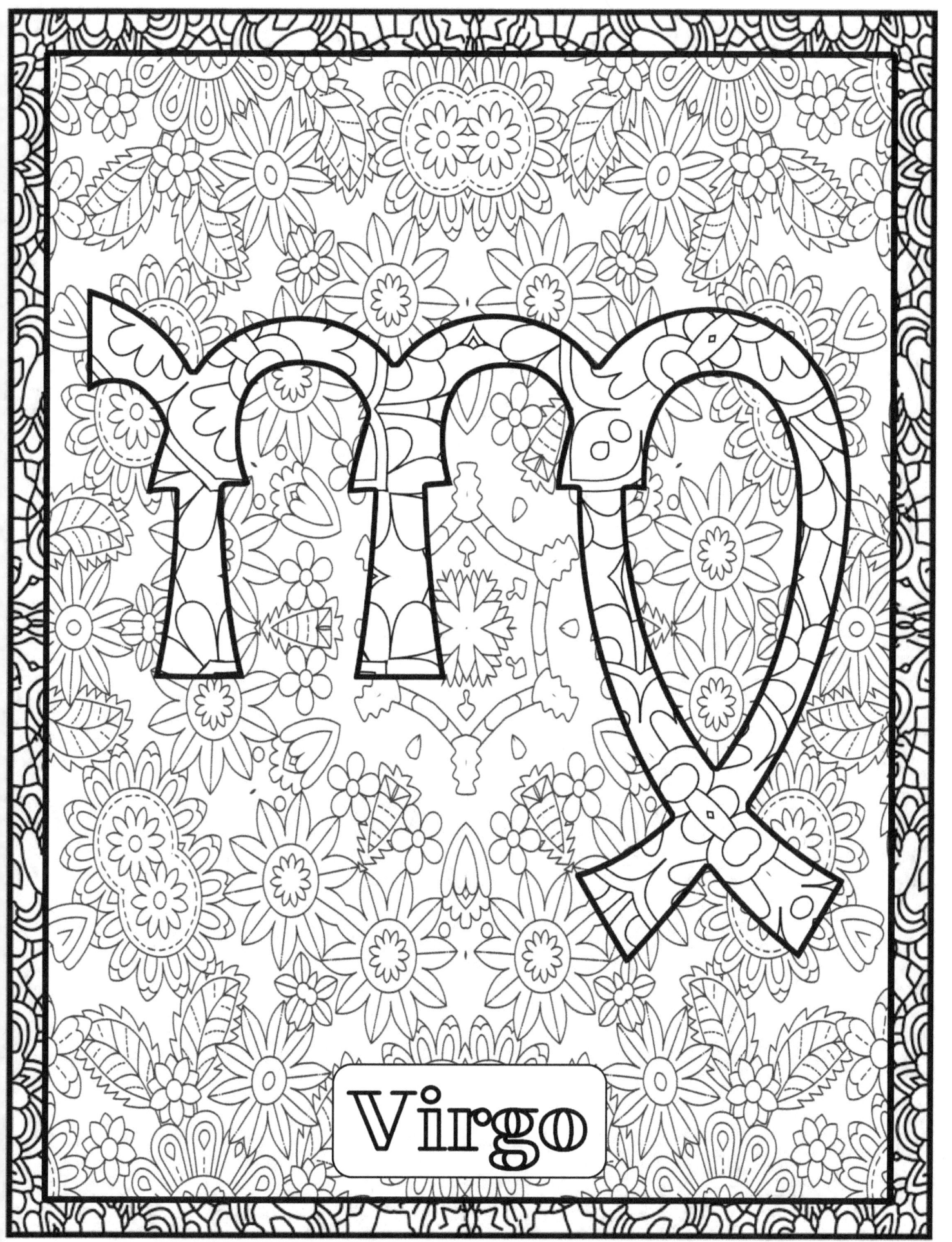

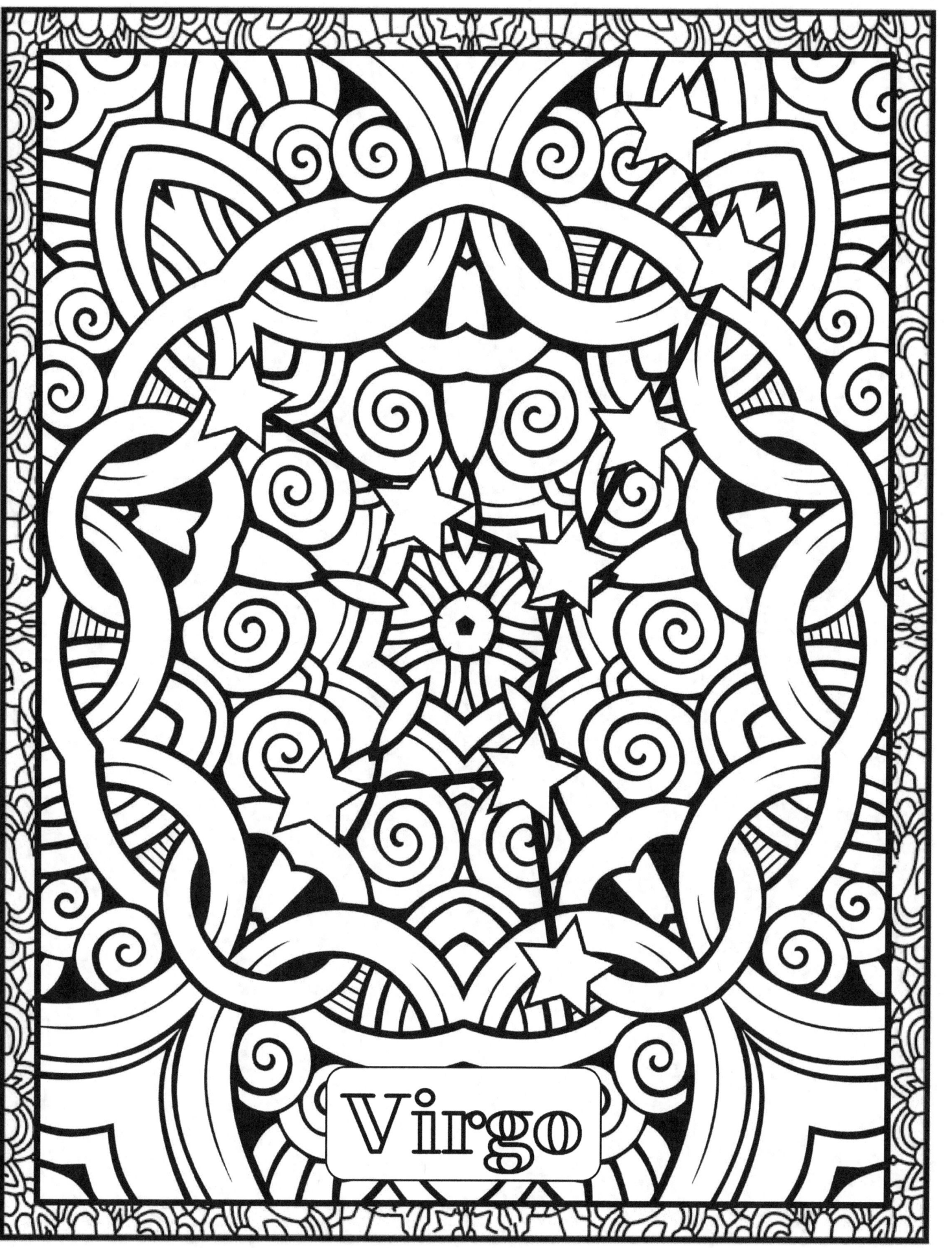

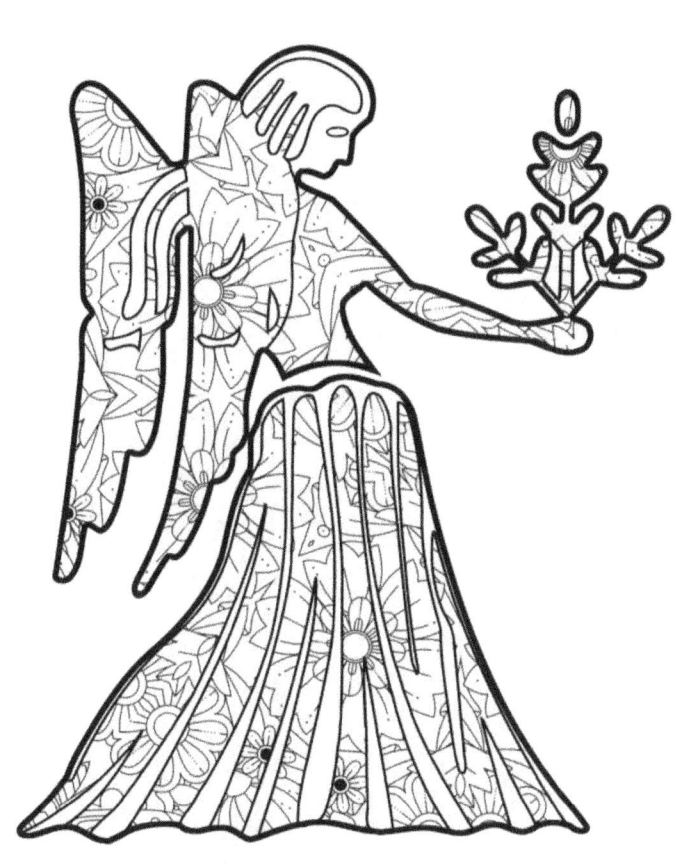

Virgo
Aug 23 – Sep 22

Practical, Loyal,
Gentle and Analytical

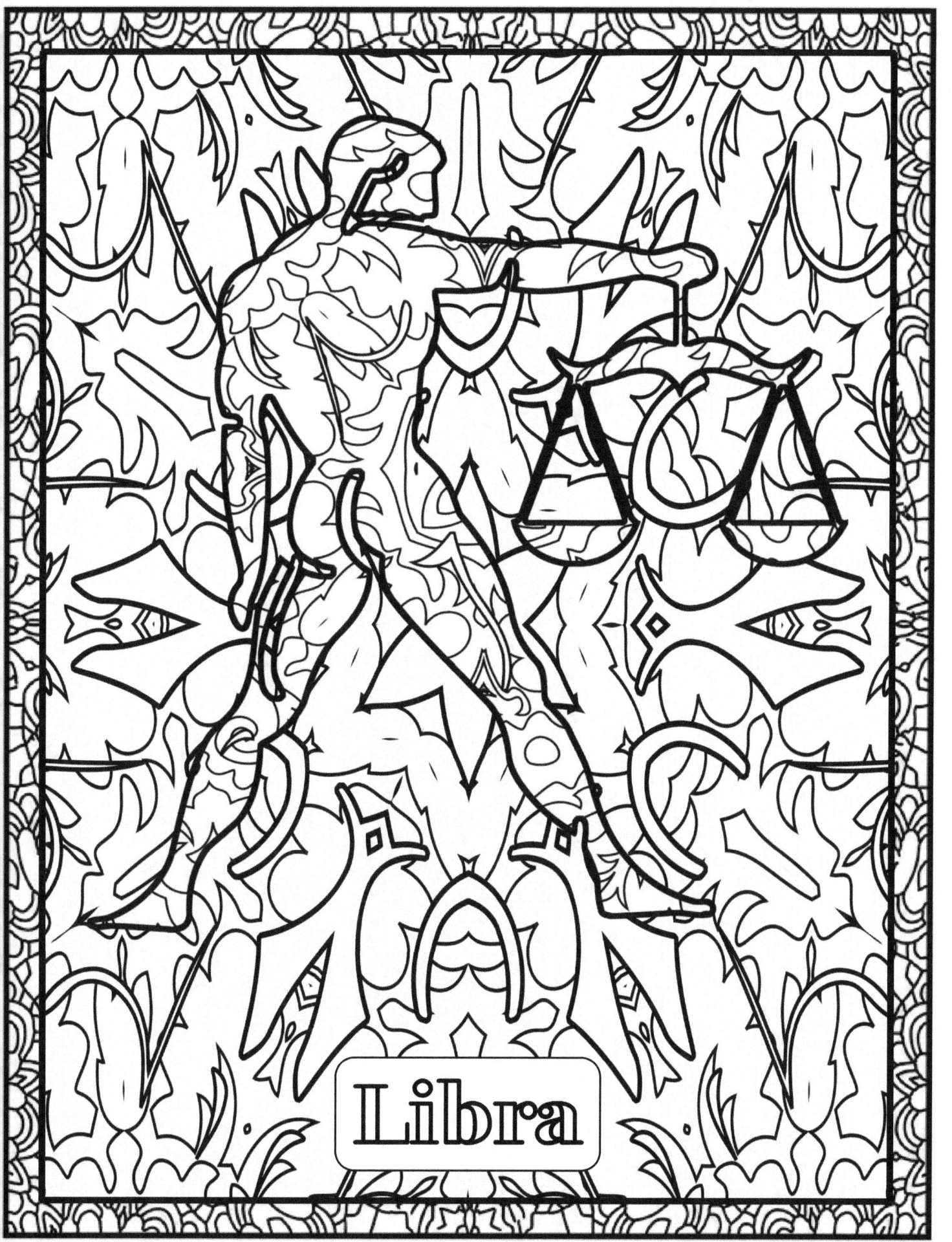

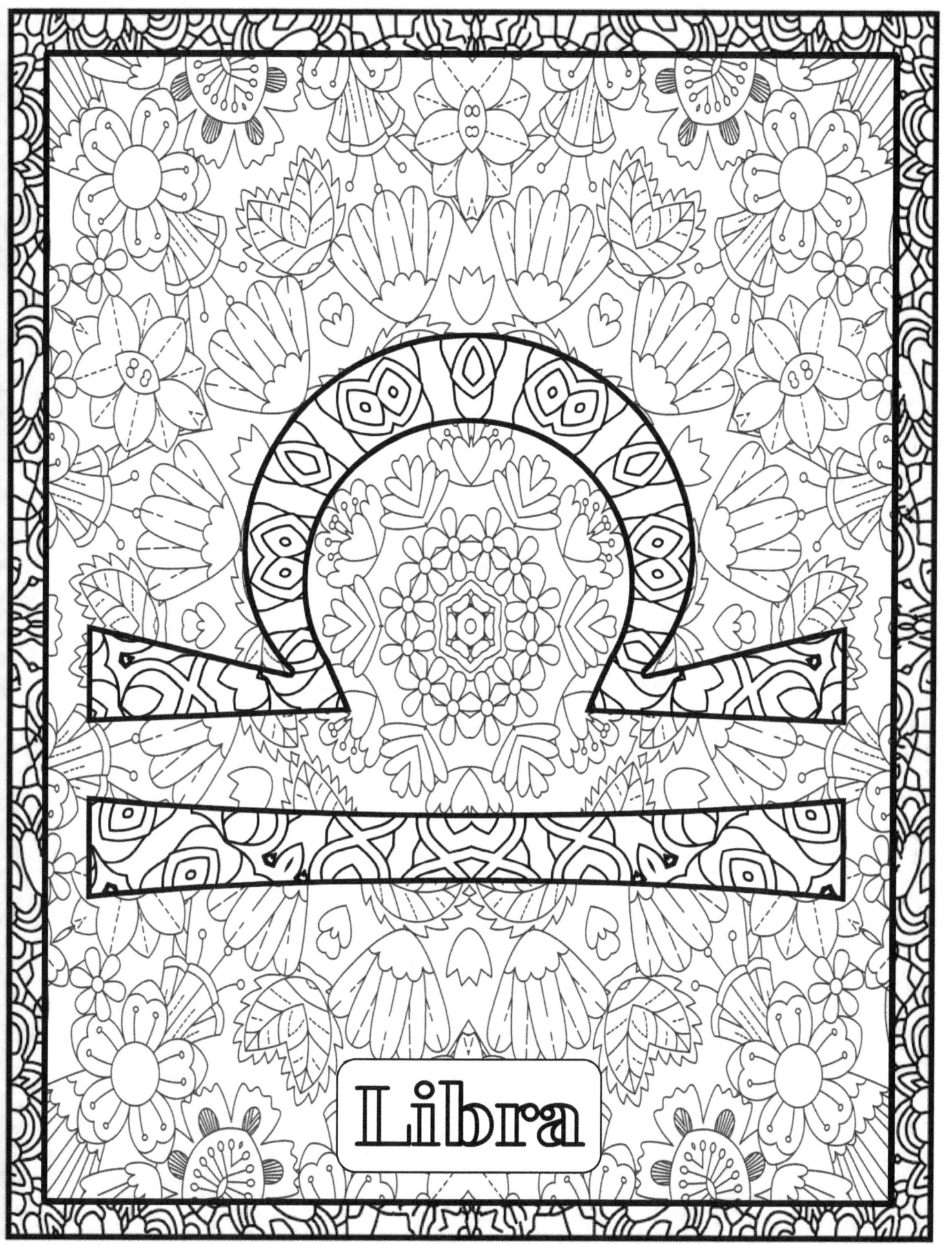

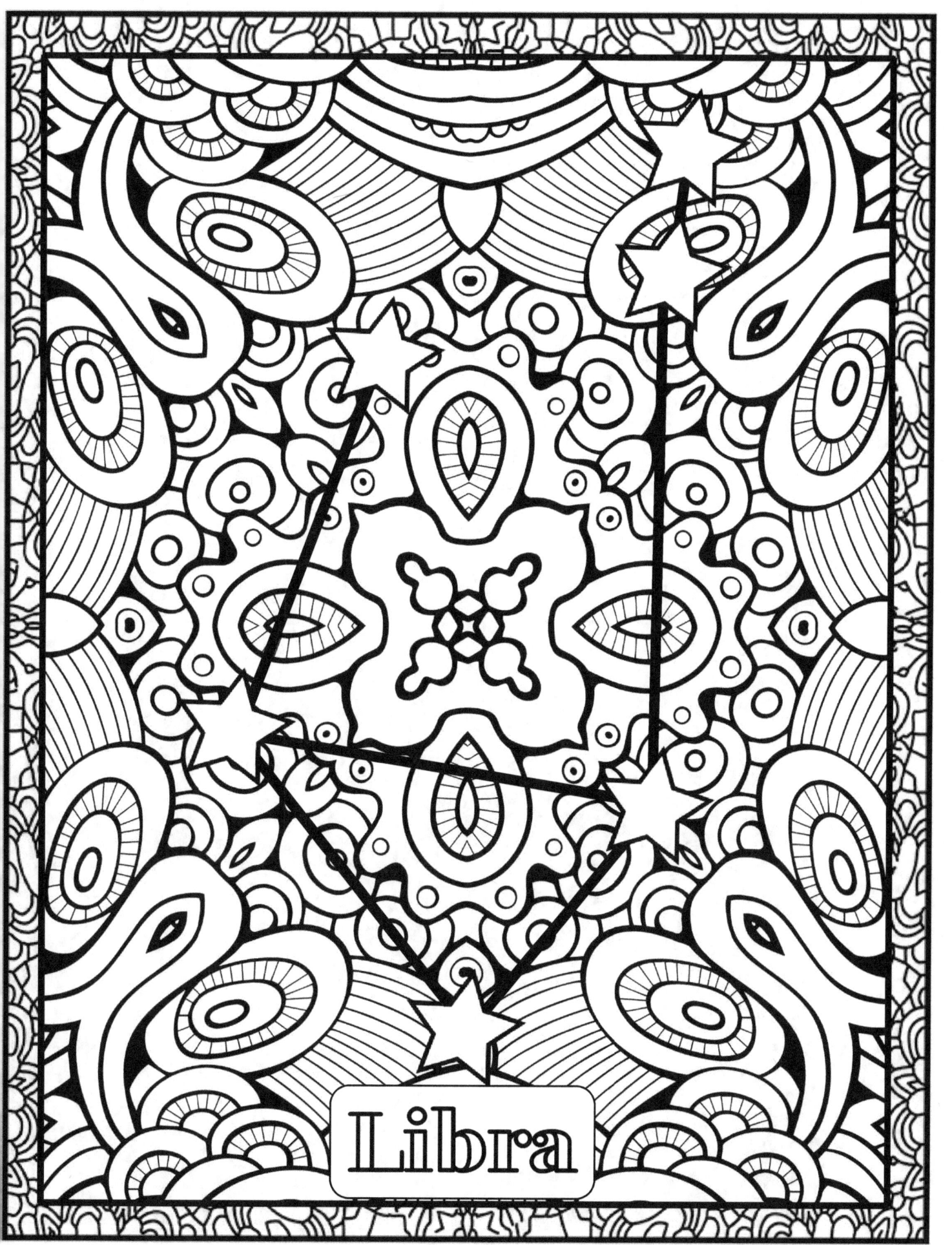

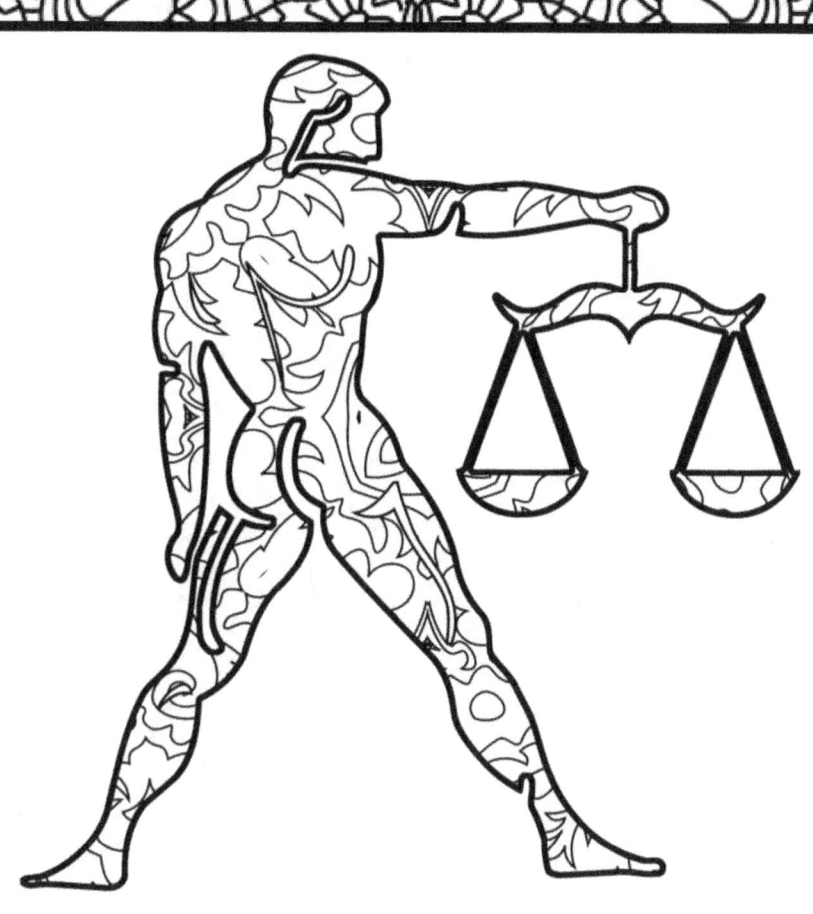

Libra

Sep 23 – Oct 22

Social, Fair-Minded, Diplomatic and Gracious

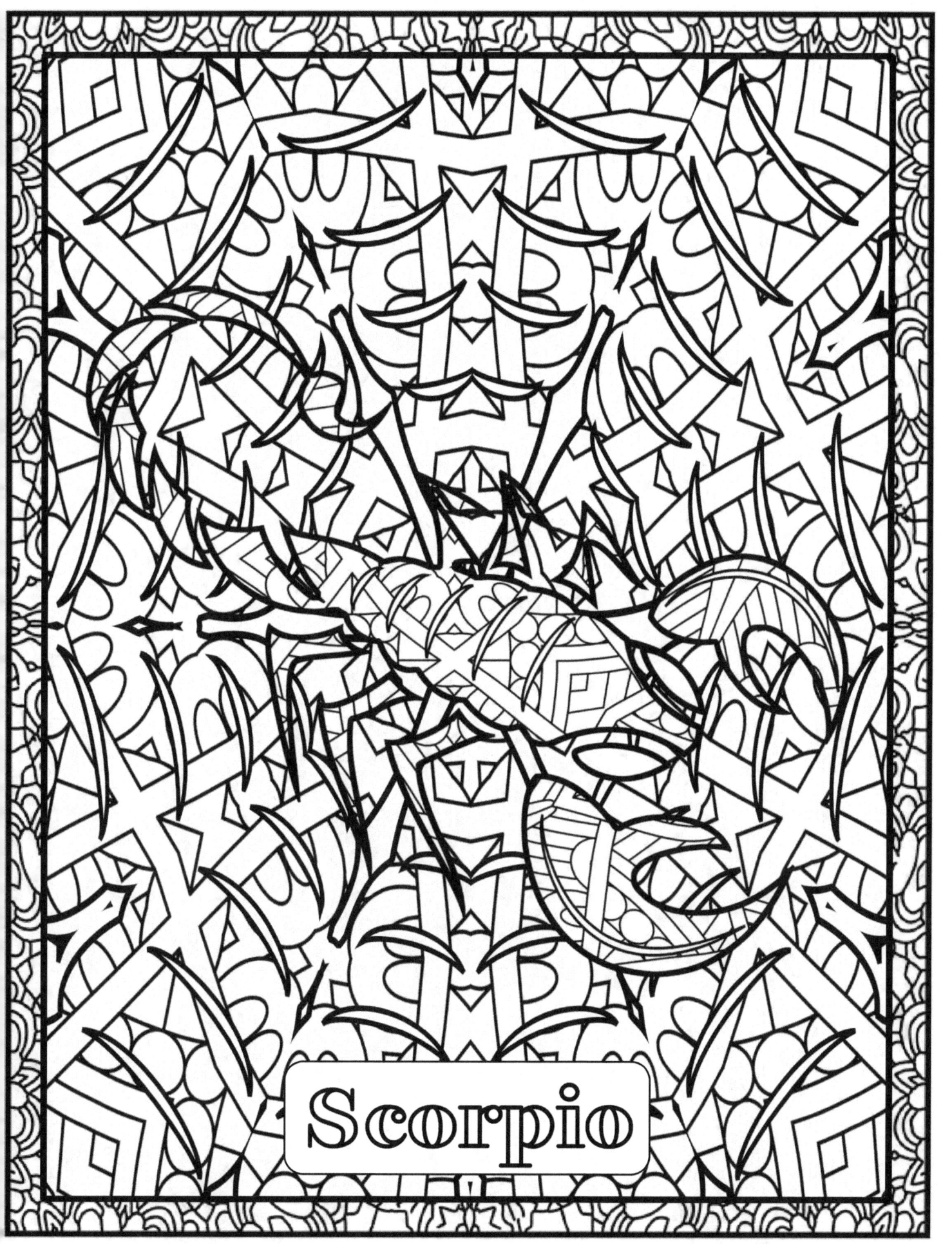

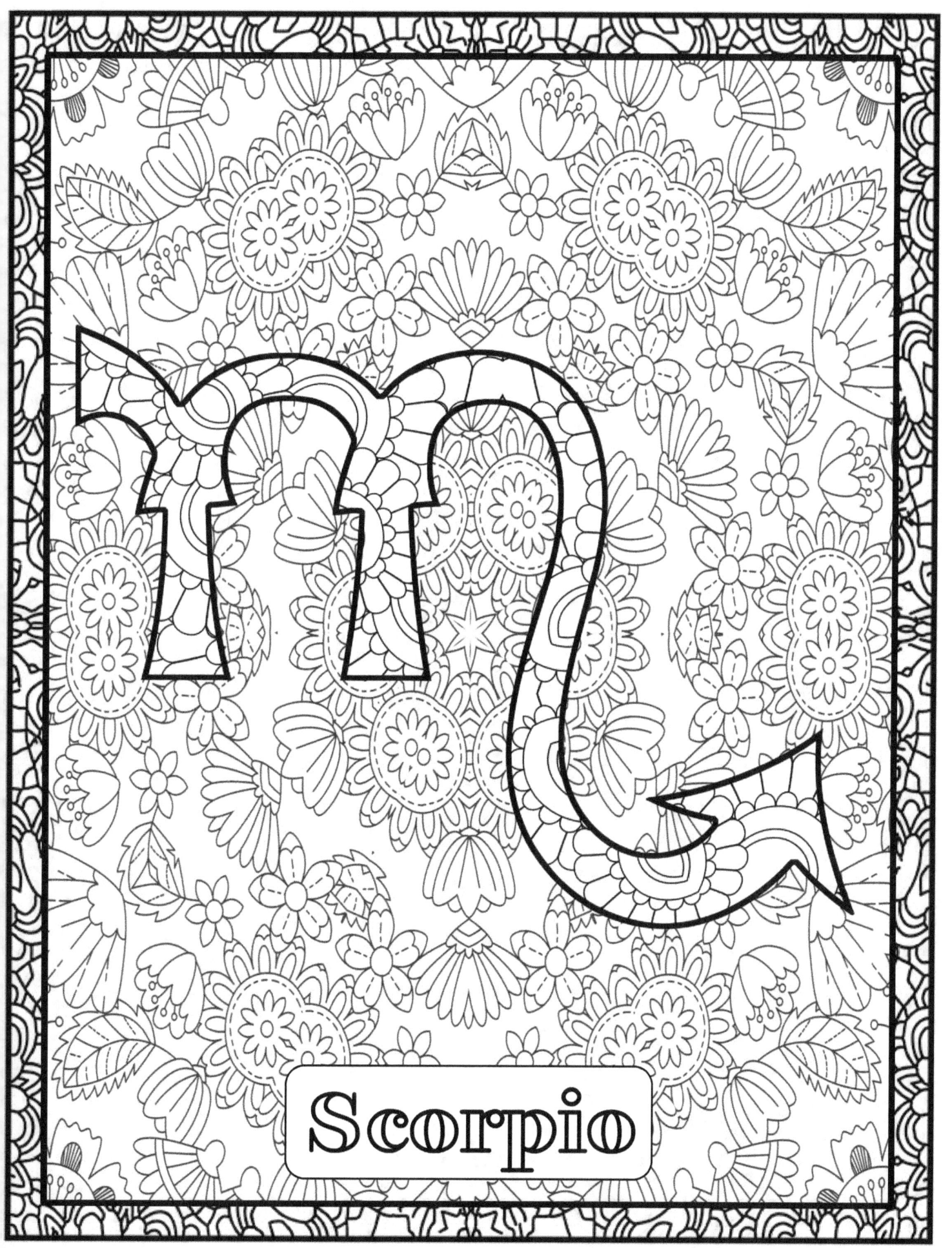

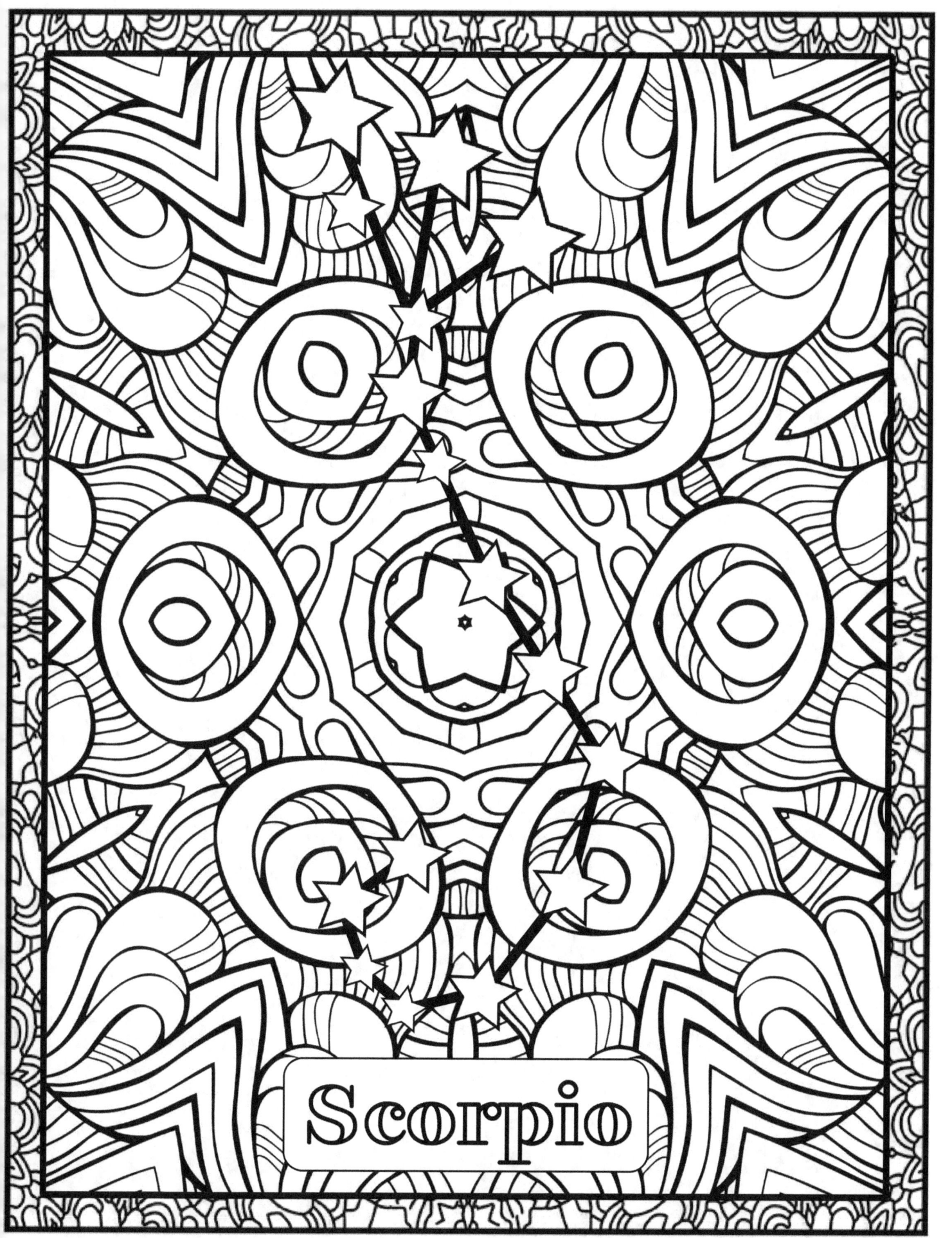

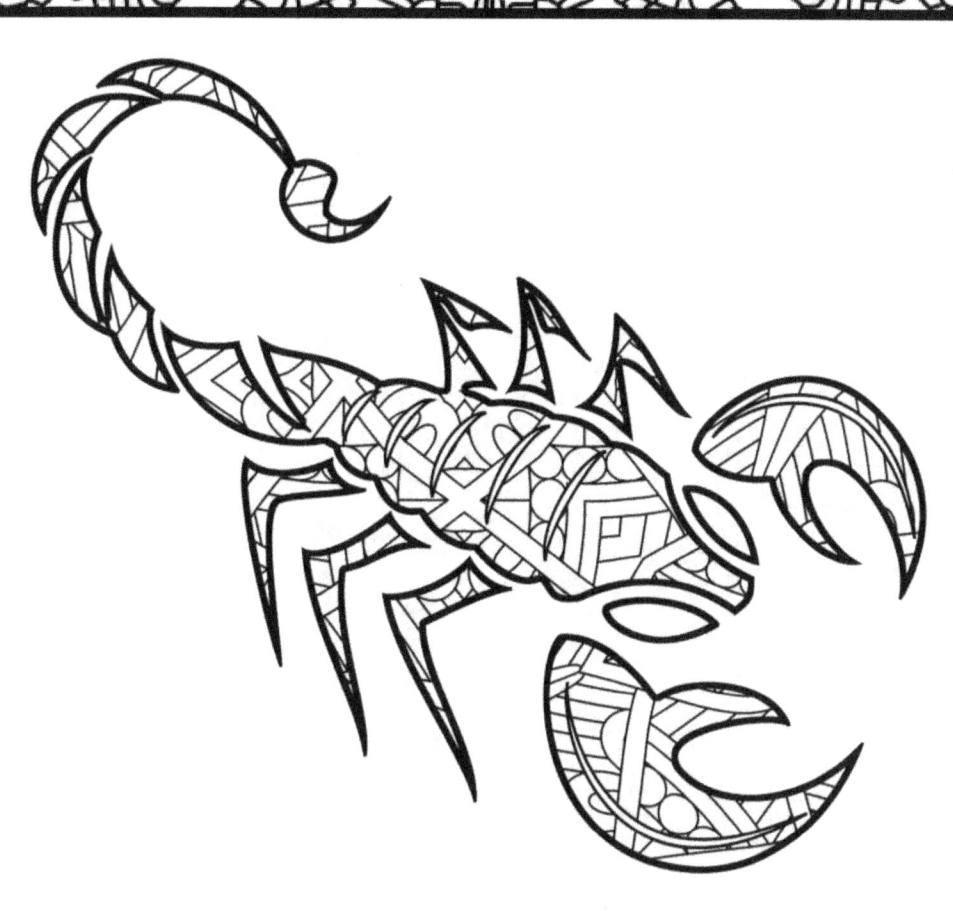

Scorpio
Oct 23 – Nov 21

Passionate, Stubborn, Resourceful and Brave

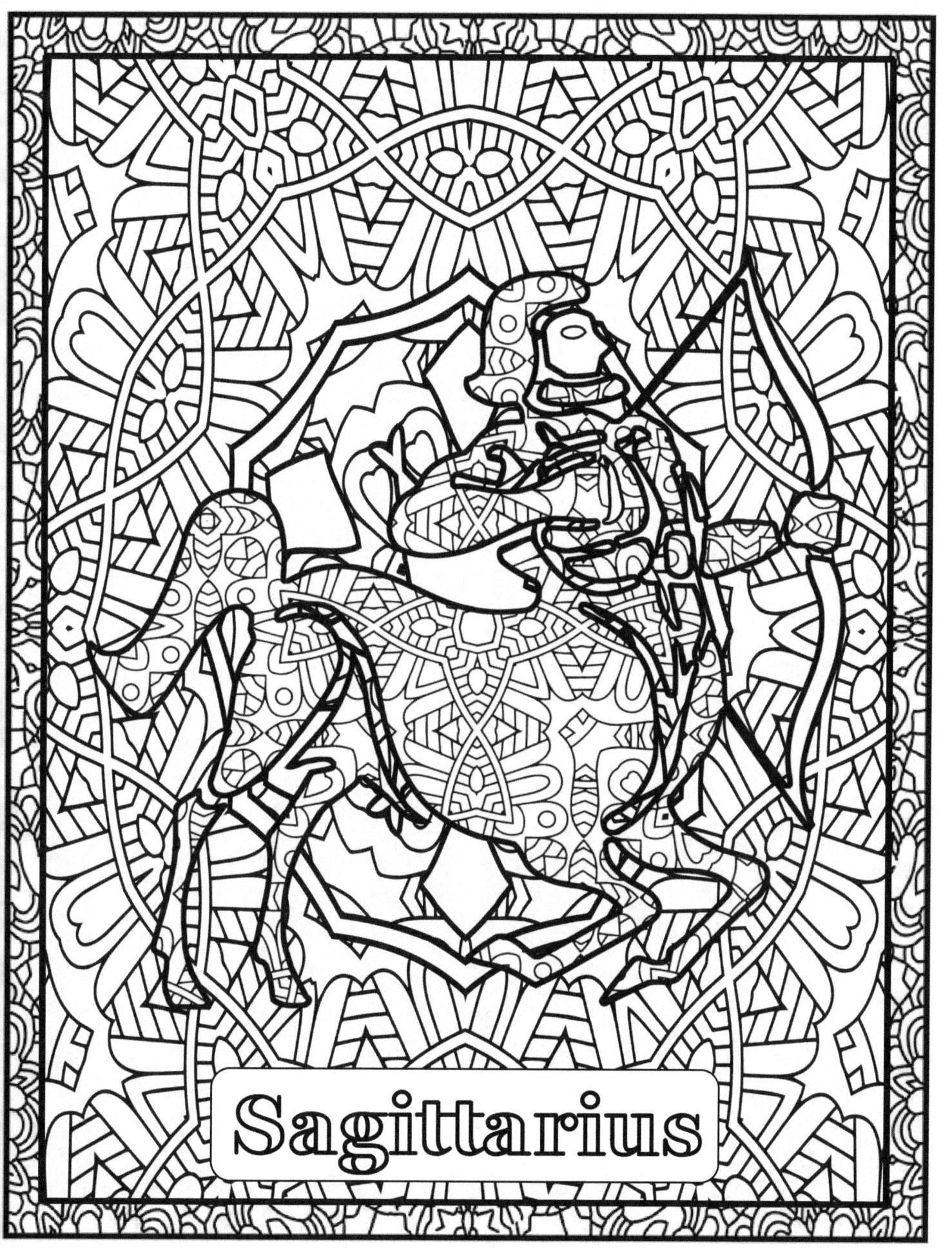

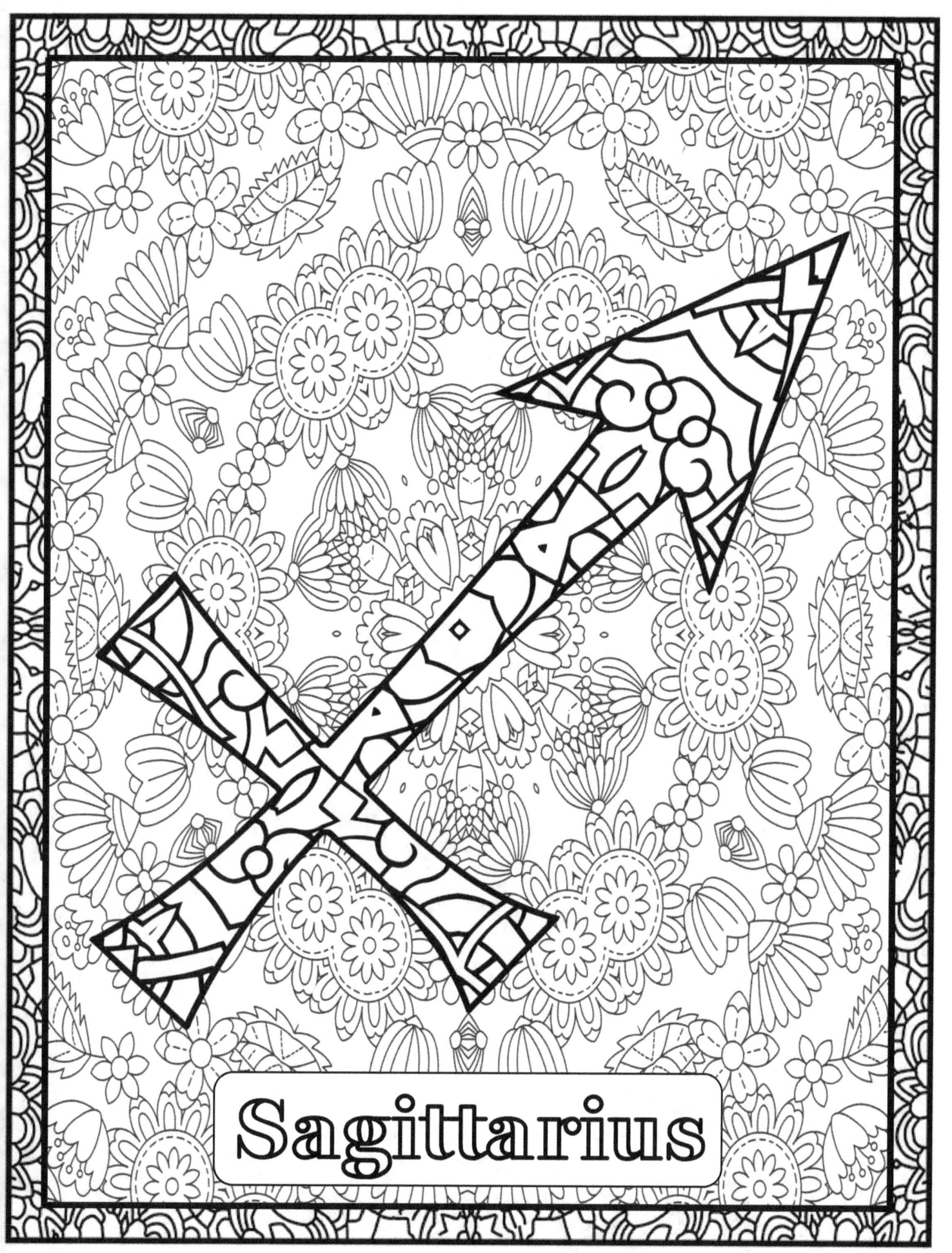

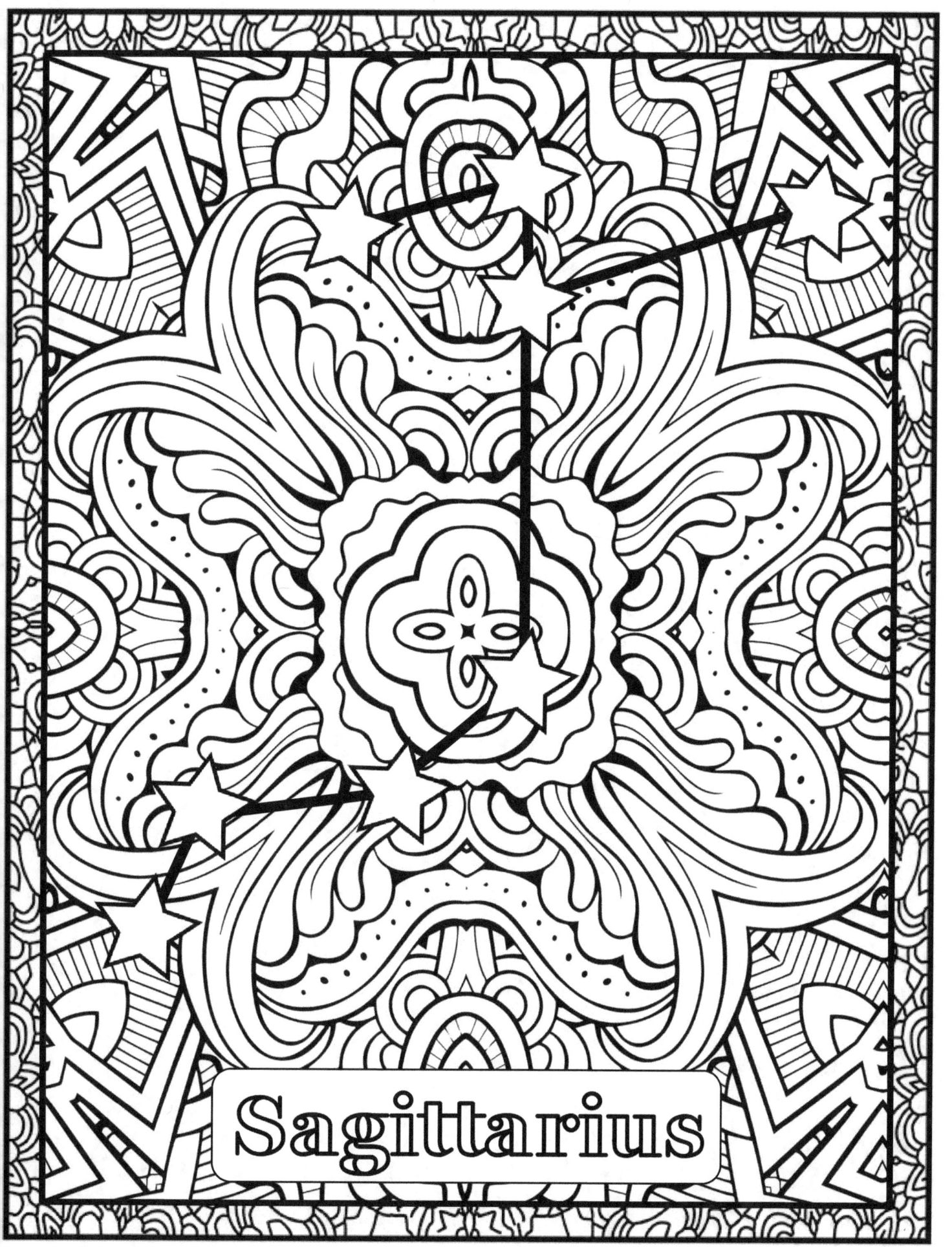

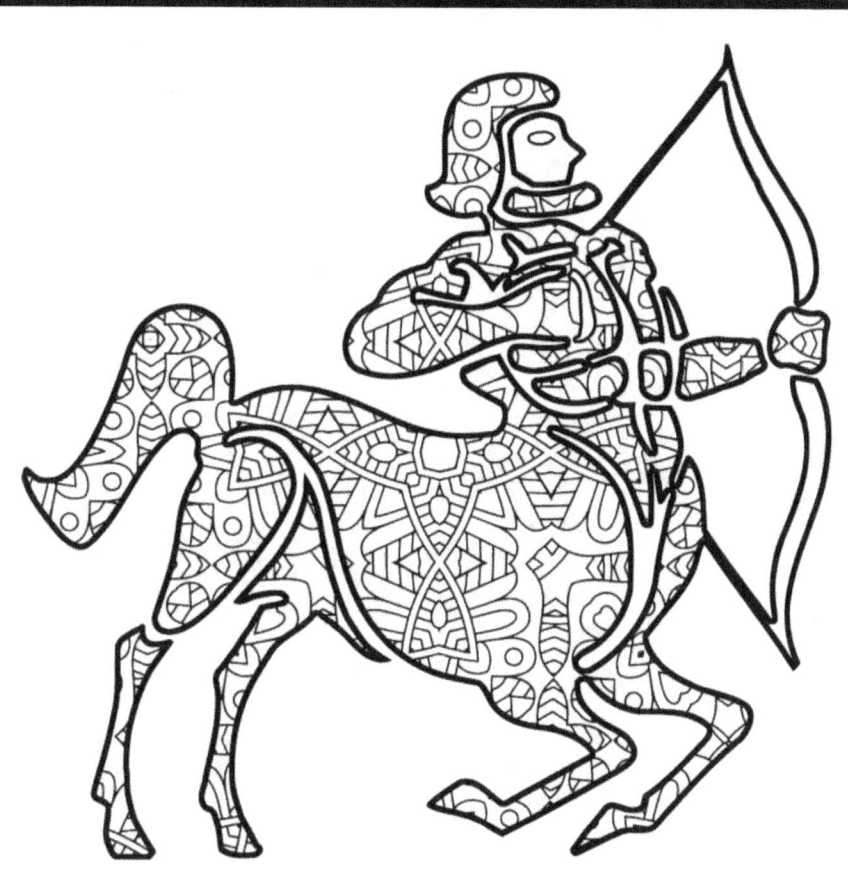

Sagittarius
Nov 22 – Dec 21

Extroverted, Optimistic, Funny and Generous

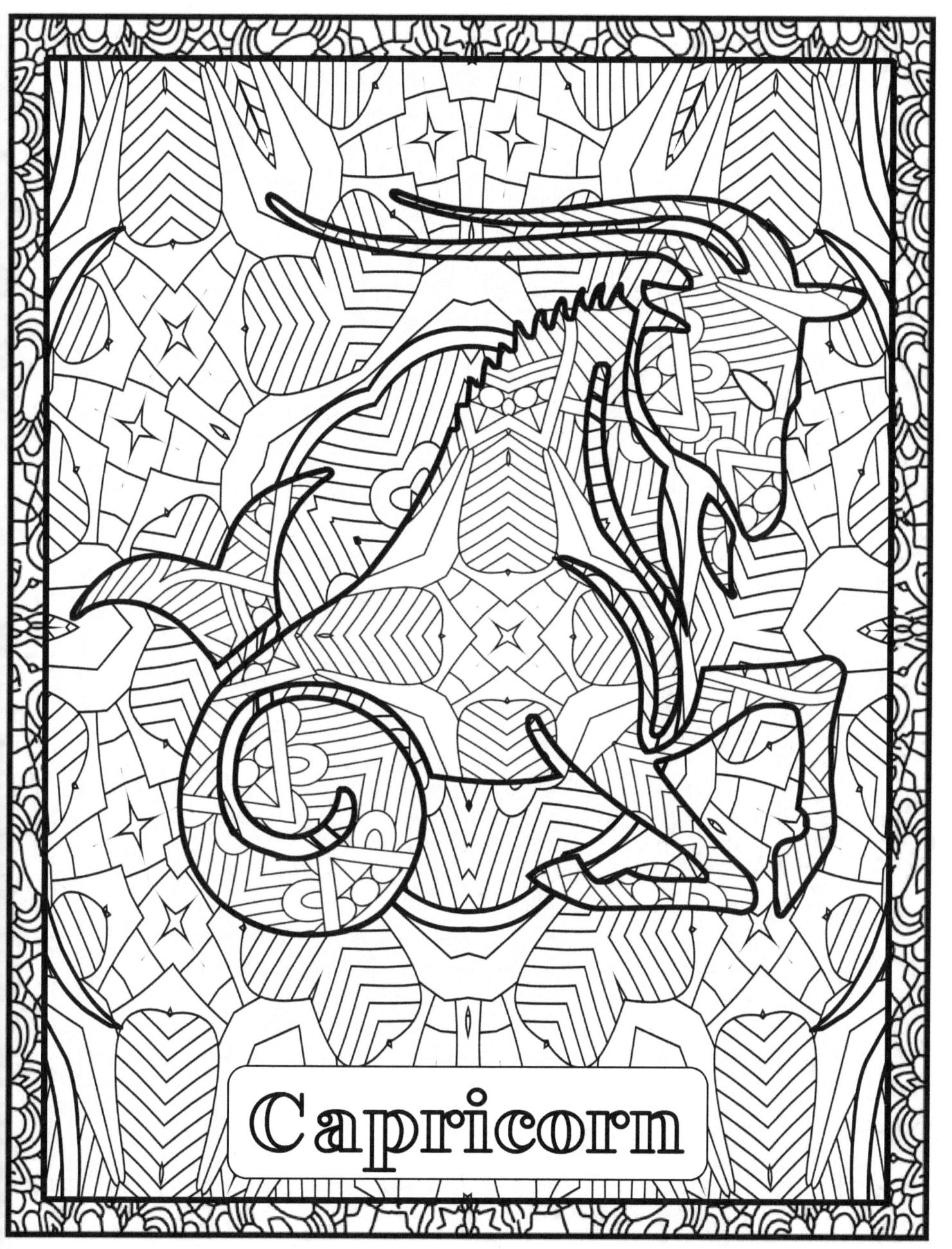

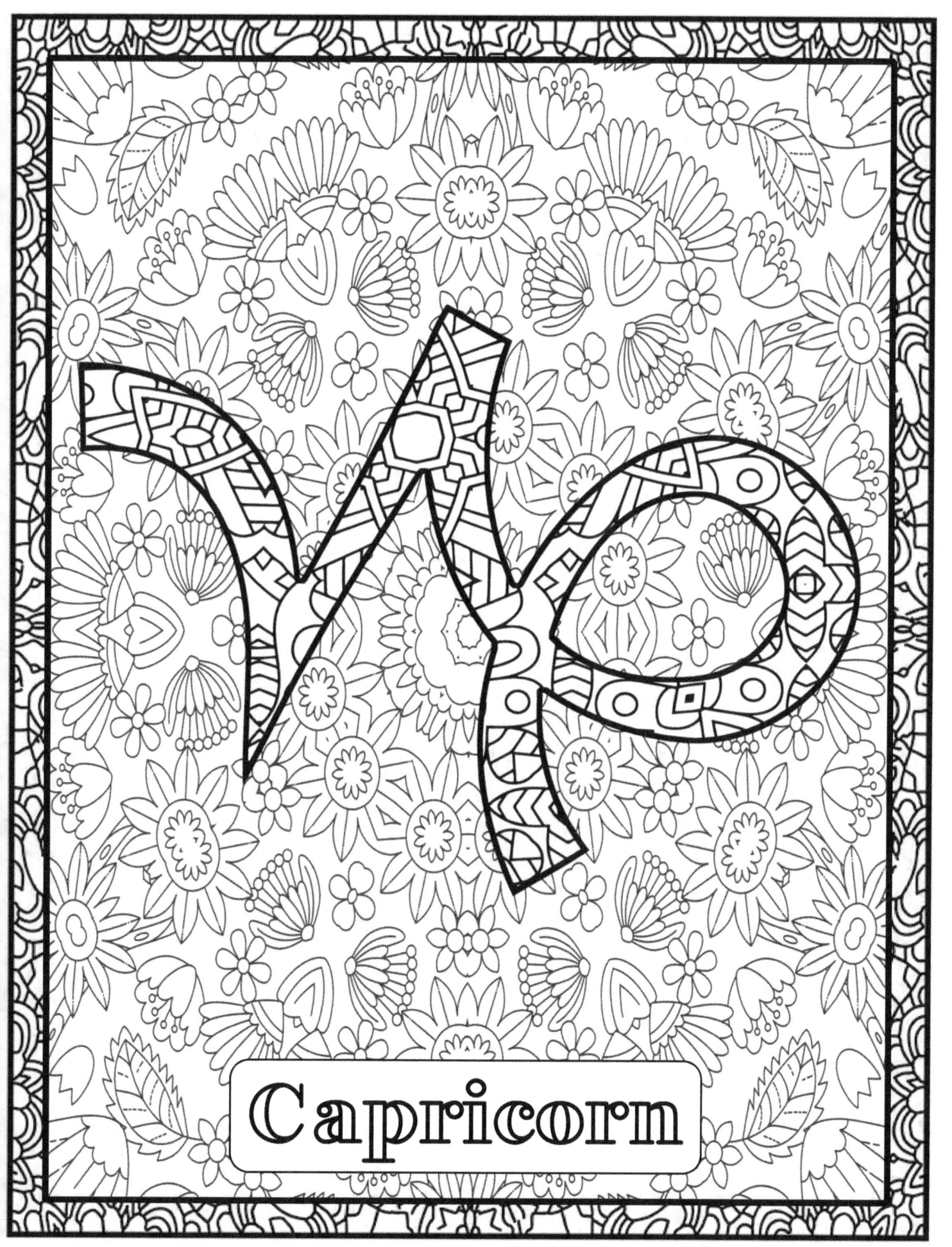

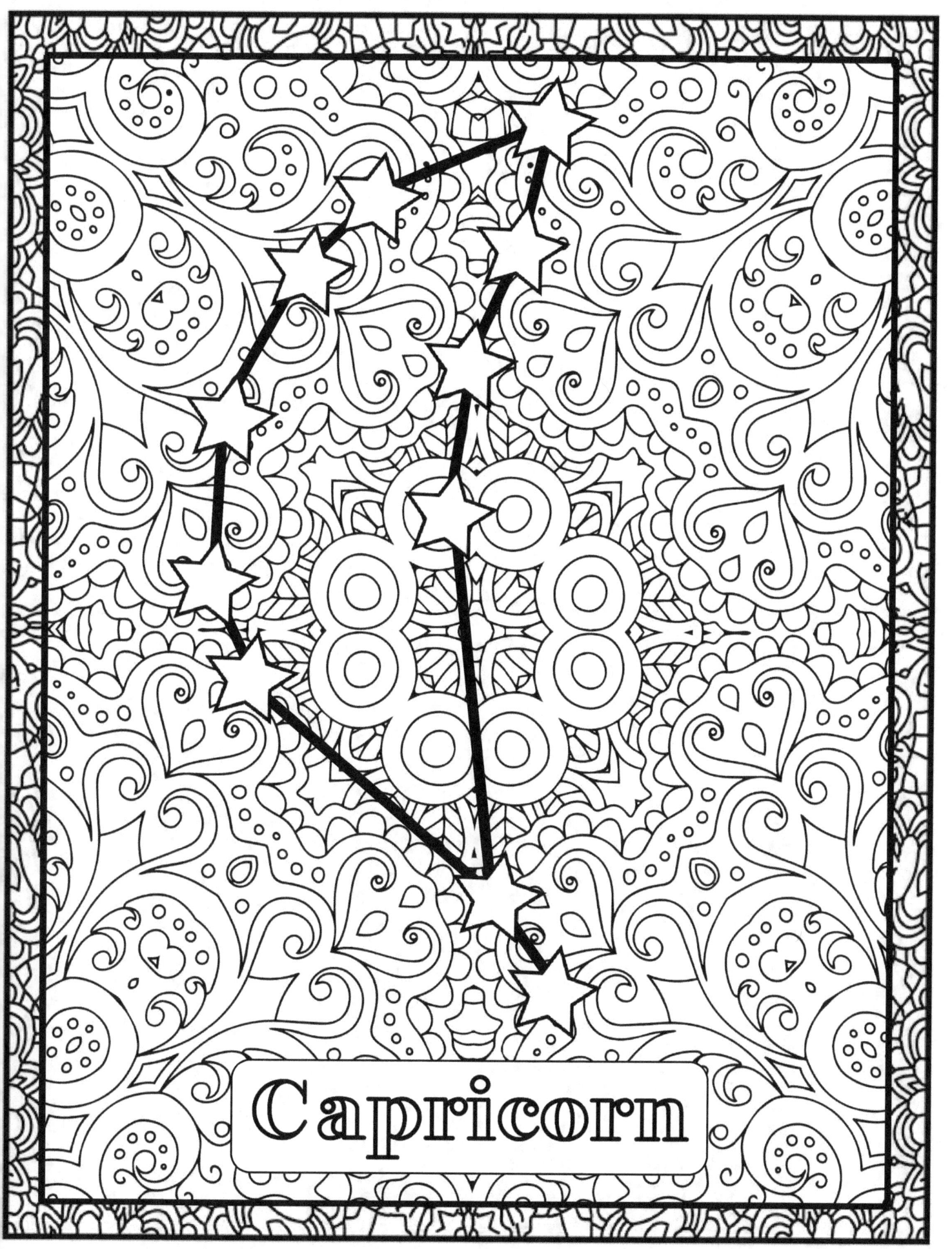

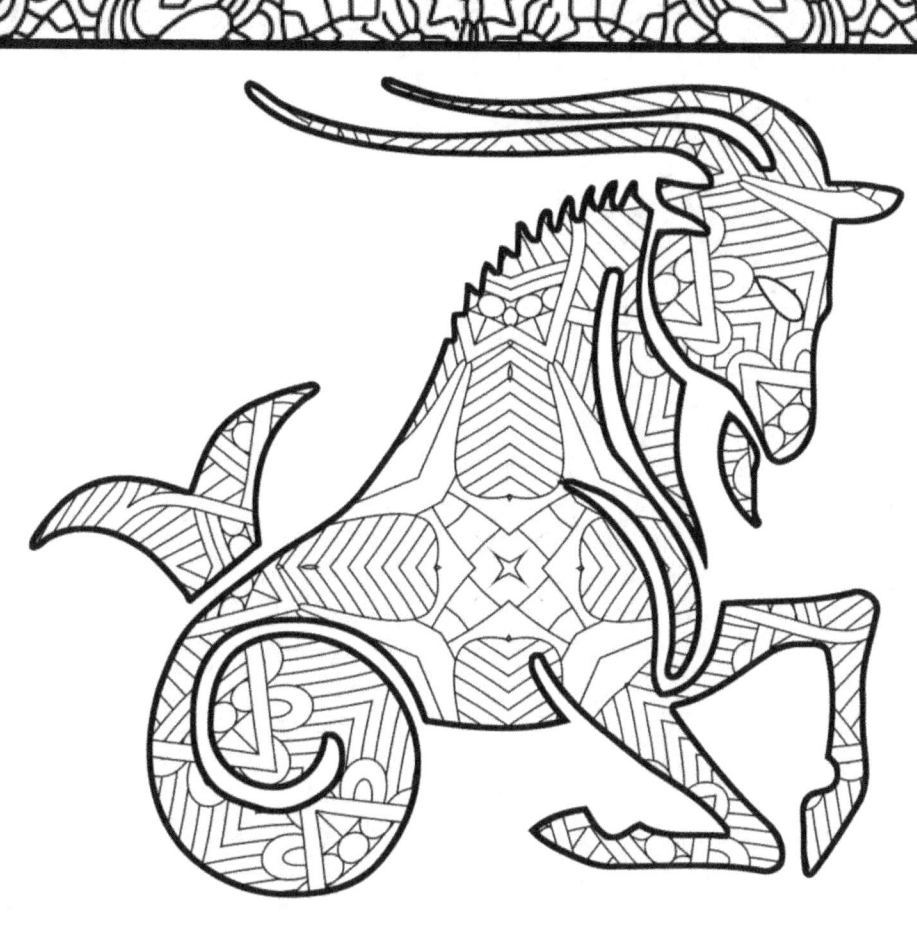

Capricorn
Dec 22 – Jan 19

Serious, Independent, Disciplined and Tenacious